THE SENTIMENTALITY OF POST-9/11 PORNOGRAPHY
FANNIE+FREDDIE

POETS
OUT LOUD

ANNIE + FREDDIE

THE SENTIMENTALITY OF POST-9/11 PORNOGRAPHY

AMY SARA CARROLL

FORDHAM UNIVERSITY PRESS *New York* 2013

Copyright © 2013 Fordham University Press

All rights reserved. No part of this publication may be reproduced, stored in a retrieval system, or transmitted in any form or by any means—electronic, mechanical, photocopy, recording, or any other—except for brief quotations in printed reviews, without the prior permission of the publisher.

Fordham University Press has no responsibility for the persistence or accuracy of URLs for external or third-party Internet websites referred to in this publication and does not guarantee that any content on such websites is, or will remain, accurate or appropriate.

Fordham University Press also publishes its books in a variety of electronic formats. Some content that appears in print may not be available in electronic books.

Library of Congress Control Number: 2012954892

Printed in the United States of America
15 14 13   5 4 3 2 1
First edition

Ricardo and Zé

LOCUTOR.— *(Al público.)* Eso prueba, una vez más, que Lupita encarna el arquetipo de la mujer mexicana: sufrida, abnegada, devota.— *(A Lupita.)* ¿Y después?
LUPITA.— *(Displicente.)* Tengo que decidir entre varias ofertas. Los productores de cine quieren que yo actúe como la protagonista de mi propio drama.
LOCUTOR.— Prácticamente es un lanzamiento al estrellato.
LUPITA.— Pero los scripts son tan . . . ¿cómo le diré? Hasta ahora ninguno me parece convincente.

TOCAYA. Presence in absence can be riveting. If I were her *tocaya*, she could read for me; but I am neither what I am nor what I should be. Always unreflective, but shimmering, shattering like a magpie or a false set of teeth. The mirror's *poke-her!* face gleams, ex‑cruciatingly unfaithful, a wind shill (negativity), the share that will not chair. the sheet,

Rosario Castellanos, *El eterno femenino*

(a seat at the table; but,
there's nothing to eat).

CONTENTS

PUBLIC POETRY PROJECT (PPP) (i) documentation ii
TOCAYA vi
Foreword by Claudia Rankine ix

ECONOMY OF GESTURE documentation (i) x———OVULATION 1———image-poems (clockwise): JUNEBUG, PERFORMANCE STUDY, SHELLSHOCKED, and SPEED QUEEN 2———THROMBOTIC 3———image-poems (clockwise): CHOOSY, GRANADA, LOST OBJECT, and STICKY 4———"THE BANALITY OF EVIL" 5———image-poems (clockwise): "All things return to Ithaca . . . ," CHEERIOS/DICTIONARY, ARROWHEAD, and "Roots and Routes" 6———LATE ONSET PARTICLE CAPITALISM 7———"THE SENTIMENTALITY OF POST-9/11 PORNOGRAPHY" 8———"Lloro cuando se quema el arroz . . ." 10———image-poems (clockwise): ZE/US, POST 9/11 (1973), PANIC ATTACK, and YOUR BREADTH 11———PETIT À PETIT 12———FAMILY PORTRAIT 13———"What Is the Difference Between Globalization and Neoliberalism?" 14———"One need not be a Chamber—to be Haunted—" 16———image-poems (clockwise): NEEDLING, AZÚCAR, LA REGLA, and OUT ON A LIMB 18———PATERNITY SUITE 19———image-poems (clockwise): PILLOW TALK, THE ZÉ BAR, and INTERIOR SCROLL 20———ARRESTED DEVELOPMENT 21———DISAPPEAR 22———SIMULTANEOUS TRANSLATION 23———HI-FI/HI-FI 2 24———PPP (v) documentation 25———FANNIE + FREDDIE 26———PPP (ii) documentation 29———INTERROGATIVE 30———INTERNATIONAL WOMEN'S DAY 2007 32———SIGN AGE SIGNAGE (*ECONOMY OF GESTURE* PROCESS NOTE and documentation [ii]) 34———POST/PAR/TUM/DOC/U/MENT 37———AFTER FACT 51———CREATIONISM 52———image-poems (clockwise): LAMENT(E), THE BEETS, OHIO, and SECRETION 53——CARAMELIZATION 54——image-poems (clockwise): "O Sage——," ?, PODS, CAST, and ALIEN ELEMENTARY 55—— ~~ANIMA SOLA~~ 56 ——~~I LOVE LUCY~~ 57——PIPE DREAM 58——A PENTAGRAM 59——WHO SHOT VALERIE SOLANAS? 60——Let's Plant a Rainbow Flag on the Moon 61 ——~~"You could put a fence around the Triangle and call it a zoo."~~ 62——CORPUS CHRISTI CORRIDO 63——HOME AGAIN, HOME AGAIN, JIGGERTY JIG/ PAPAPAPÁ/FINIAL FILIAL 64—— SOCIAL DRAMA 65——REDEMPTION SONG 66——PARALLAX 67——image-poems (clockwise): LACKEY, MANTIS, and O! 68—— ~~A LOVE LETTER AS~~ LOUSY AS A COLD 69——WONDERS TAKEN FOR SIGNS/Filthy Minds Feed Filthy Mouths 70——image-poems (clockwise): COMMONWEALTH, SHADOW BOX, HAIKU, and indecision 71—— ~~LIKE A CANARY~~ IN A COLD MIND 72——PPP (iv) documentation 73—— SWARM: 74——TRANSPATENTRY 75——image-poem "CADA HORA/ MÁS VERDE" 76——TINA MODOTTI'S "WONDERFULL" 78——*WHEN PLATITUDES BECOME FORMS* 82——A (corn) 83——~~"I HATE BREEDERS"~~ 84—— BUILT ENVIRONMENTAL –ISMS 85——"ECONOMISTS DO IT WITH MODELS" 86——*TRANS*PARENT (I & II) 87——EUREKA 88——PROSE/ CONS 89—— *ECONOMY OF GESTURE* documentation (iii) 90

Acknowledgments 91

FOREWORD

Claudia Rankine

In Amy Sara Carroll's *FANNIE + FREDDIE/The Sentimentality of Post-9/11 Pornography*, jokes, puns, riddles, platitudes, hackneyed phrases, adages, boilerplate, buzzwords, mottos, proverbs, rubber stamp rhetoric, slogans, threadbare phrases, trite remarks, and truisms layer each other to provide a portrait of our contemporary American landscape as experienced by working- and middle-class Americans. Carroll, using her own birth story and parenting partnership, chronicles—through prose poems, images, and medical documents—the "conciliatory constellation(s)," to repeat her phrase, that exist alongside the precarity of "real life." This challenging collection enacts the clarity of the triteness of contemporary optimism in light of the lack of response during Katrina, the subprime mortgage crisis, the absence of a national healthcare system, the economic crash, U.S.-Mexico border relations—to name only a few of the realities Carroll references. Throughout this stunningly complex and moving portrayal, the lyric resides in the intimacy of the connection of mother to son, the music lives on, in the attachment of members of a family, despite everything. "There's something vindictive about the family romance," Carroll writes. It is "kinship akin to anonymity" in a capitalistic economy that "in the end is the only game in town." The intelligence, compassion, and dimensionality of this collection place it in a category all its own—it belongs to and is crafted out of the psychic anxieties of the twenty-first century. I, for one, was both exhilarated and humbled by *FANNIE + FREDDIE/The Sentimentality of Post-9/11 Pornography.*

OVULATION, egg-drop dense as Ovaltine, all the afore mothers I cannot be. Low Sunday brew destined to scorch the lungs' pod-dwelling fronds. Midwifery, remodeling a planetarium's bottlecap or bottle-bottom heavy lens, I turn upon myself. This June, a Gemini germinates in my mind, ~~twin exclamation (!!)~~ marks a find, *bijiminy* bigeminy. Tone-deaf crickets serenade me, ~~*The corn, knee-high, kneads a whippin'*~~. Meanwhile, the Jim Crow itch that knows no scratch pardons the sky for the clouds that pass, the miles—adulterous hours—the calendar's ex. ~~*Should I stay or should I go*~~? Thick discharge, papers glow with news of an aftermath. And, every sign I think I see, malapert malaprop, misdirects me to the carriage house, a round back (Quasimodo's vanishing act). *Now you see them, now you don't.* Two light sabers, a double yolk. A sulfurous pill lodges itself. Beneath the tongue. Against my will, doubled-over, ~~womb-hungry, the birds of regret worm-hole entry~~. Tracks of a plane—*long time coming*—trail off, a dissident text, messaging, *A house in order needs no past.* ~~Sheer righteousness, broken glass.~~

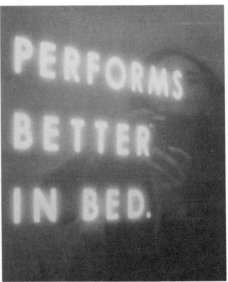

THROMBOTIC

~~Excuse me,~~ I need to speak to a man about a horse. *Do you mean you're going to whiz like a wild beast?* No, I'm off to converse with a woman about a chameleon, a meatier breech of contract (contractions' being the subjunctive substance of robot-human contact). A mouth-watering hole, exact change, a home-grown, elemental earthiness to which "we"— *check their IDs*—are bound. The world spins 'round its axis, night and day, time's foreplay, played out on our faces and hands. Crow's feet, some stickler's sweet sound of the *muzak*'s occlusion ~~(one partially occluded vein, a thrombotic disorderly, rushing to and fro~~, divided midstream, an ocean's expanse now turned mighty river). Is our Dog capable of Kafka's luminescent levitation? Light as a feather, stiff as a board, when I touch your lever, it's the untruths I abhor. ~~Not white lies, not brown cocks crowing thrice to unlock the sanctity of a shifting moral plateau.~~ No, the levees broke, the authority choked on the cuckoo in the clock. *Do you mean Sylvester swallowed Tweety?* Not exactly. The devil's in the details, the proof's in the punch, the bird, like the hand, is in the bush, and this story's meteor missed high ground.

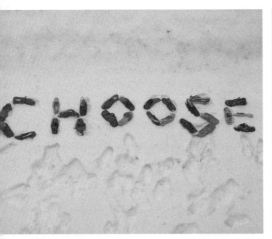

"THE BANALITY ~~OF EVIL~~"

Why did the chicken cross the road? There's something vindictive about the family romance, ~~which comes on swiftly like an asthma attack. I don't want to make any necessary moves, only what's wanton, frivolous.~~ I've been framed; I want to step out of the limelight, to slit the neck of the night, to slip the noose of the moon's cock-eyed camera. It's bearing down on me and I need for you to make, believe that ~~I imagined something~~ Otherworldly. Not the stranglehold of triangulation, but kinship akin to anonymity, the quiet currant, cordial as History (a gentleman's caller, kinder than calamity). Not the continuous erasure of anomaly, which, fortifying the heart, paradoxically piques the lock, Smith's prurience. Propriety ~~(keepin' up with the Joneses)~~: *The Sun Also Rises*. "Go Down Moses." A coat of arms rarely fits, let alone flatters its constituents—all-hand-me-downs and left feet—I trip the wire to cross the street.

LATE ONSET ~~PARTICLE CAPITALISM~~

~~Strike when the iron is hot:~~ the spot bubbles to the surface—red-faced—some malicious, illicit strawberry, singed below a soft cap of hair, I discover it there by accident, demand an explanation. Vague mumblings of *scalp stimulation, postpartum emotion in high gear*. I dream of an embedded chip, my son's induction into the matter market. What matters is this: *He is okay*. Well, temporarily. Weeks later, the market crashes, so to speak—in the ER, we become parental footnotes while the real work is done—intubation, a central line, the social worker in talcum tones. The doctor lays down her hand, a pack of worst case scenarios that fan out across the table. ~~He may not make it through the night and if he does we cannot predict the extent of the "devastation."~~ Devastation? ~~Loss of limbs, loss of hearing, loss of vision, permanent brain damage, multiple organ failure.~~ Unable to process listing-as-event, I adhere to my own paranoid versions of the tale: They are removing the chip, deactivating the product. He temporarily is checked into an upscale refurbishing clinic. On a respirator to regain consciousness, he manufactures nipple dreams, which intersect with my own fantasies of his lopsided smile, an escape-artist's grin. ~~In other words: recycling lines pared out to me, choking on their saccharine-sweet cadences,~~ I wish first that he might live and then greedily branch out to demand additional reassurance. The white-coated herds that hoard expertise like pocket change prove all too accommodating, commodity-trading interpellation: ~~late onset GBS, bacterial meningitis,~~ each one of us, a Petri dish, navigating the birth canal.

7

"THE SENTIMENTALITY OF POST-9/11 PORNOGRAPHY"

I swear by Christ—the greatest socialist in history. *Fighting for peace is like fucking for virginity.* Yesterday, I learned that the Russian word for cabaret literally means "theatre of miniatures." It's hard to imagine an epoch in which Church and State officials interchangeably had the audacity to value the merits of quantifying how many angels could dance on the head of a pin. ~~Well, kind of, but, not really. Some things are best left to the imagination.~~ *Your Gaze Hits the Side of My Face.* Picture forty, an arrivant, crisp, squeaky-clean, as thunder. Not sudden or shocking, but what seemed necessary after the air's sticky treacherousness. Formerly informative, but thick as maternity (universal, remote). The couch slumps (defeat's feat propped up), capitulates to Progress' fiber optics. He claims, *I don't quite view it as the broken egg; I view it as the cracked egg.* Since when did the average-Joe pretend that a cracked egg didn't portend a dire situation? **Amigo, whichever way the wind blows, my heart's harbor jams the signal**—a murmur, a currant, Event, a riptide. "Suite as marmalade," she replied. *It's complicated.* ~~Like: Go-Fish wish fulfillment, naner-technology (as in *Yes, we have no bananas . . .*) Can the obvious bear Being (repeated)? *If it's not broke, don't fix it.* I need you like a whole in my head, the migraine-angle of a master narrative. *El perfil del hombre . . .* the righteous shall inherit the emperor's flashy new duds.~~ Your touch snags the stocking (I used to rob the cradle), the atmosphere sinking, bankrolled as a fable. Buffet flat. Broke. It's three below. And, somebody is sure to know somebody, who let herself go open an umbrella indoors. Modest, yet respectable, I am a romantic—"through and through"—each morn I vow to undo the ties that bind. ~~It's hard to find good help. *Let Us Now Praise Famous Men.* Come again—was it egg-on-your-face or the chicken-crossing that led on your leading ladies to captivate me with their obsolete technologies (of gender, of capture)?~~ I dream: "The Sentimentality of Post-9/11 Pornography" circulates as required reading. I wander between D.F. crumbling department stores, mumbling, ~~*All I wanted was a pair of genes.*~~ If the gait is the signature's destiny, put a pebble in your glass slipper and make-believe it's a disguise. Frenetic as the visible, the century's airtight alibi inscribes itself on the forehead of the aforementioned pin. On a dime, I'd jump into bed, steal the thunderous clap of realism. *Life's a revolver more stringent than fiction.* And, my favorite fantasy micro-lends your conviction Sade's monotonous drone. Come hell or highwater, it's murky to own: Loch Ness rears a monster, lakes empty the sea, globally warming up to the lies that lie in store for us. ~~Is a nanopoetics phonetic enough? *Ya basta.* Why are all the questions rhetorical (and, all the answers interfaced) when truth's a bloody bastard in the Elysian killing fields of~~ "Taxation w/o Representation"? Poster-child of Babel, bring on your latest depravity, a land, mine, C.O.D.—*you get what you pay for* and you pay for the rite to be—a citizen.

"Lloro cuando se quema el arroz..."

It's been said there are two kinds of women. The first set ponders, *What does he see in her?* The second set remasters conjecture, *What does she see in a he?* If you make friendly overtures toward either, expect the following scenarios to unfold like lawn chairs or card tables. Invite the former over for dinner, she will excuse herself mid-meal, go to the restroom, and, quiet as a church mouse, inspect your housekeeping. Invite the latter out for a drink, she'll assume your unconscious has gotten the better of you. ~~She'll remind herself that the role of the initiator sucks, but, nevertheless (somebody had to do it), will relish the prospect of stage-blocking the Conquest for days to come. Are you fed up with my generalizations?~~ The week before last a man had the nerve to observe in mixed company, *Feminism is obsolete.* I asked (desperately attempting to channel Adrian Piper circa *My Calling [Cards] #1 and #2*), *What's the point you're trying to make?* My righteous indignation did not improve my person. ~~For a long time, I was troubled by my niece's nickname—Isla. I mentioned my concern to a friend, *Why are folks in the habit of compromising their daughters from Day 1? I mean I also have an abiding affection for our suffering Ladies, but, I'd think twice before naming a daughter Dolores, Soledad, Isla . . .~~* He raised an eyebrow at me to pluck isling praises. Thank you, I stand corrected. *No man is an island*, but, a strong, independent woman, caught in History's jetstream becomes her own streaming media, restorative behavior, a force to be reckoned with, both landed and set adrift. Rosario Castellanos wrote, "Debe haber otro modo de ser." She also electrocuted herself in a bathtub. Accidental suicide? "El eterno feminino"? ~~Spike my tea with the oxymoronic, lead me down the Garden's bifurcating paths, pump my subprime. Popcorn colonels wreak havoc with my crown. Kahlo caló—cognitive dissonance—Kahlúa harbors comparable ambivalence (53-proof caffeination). And, this raw hide?~~ From one woman to the next, I commend your keening sense of observation, your flare for a theatre of the absurd. Twenty thousand leagues under the sea, I wear my whiteness uneasily for Reason our fair, generic She could never imagine.

ZE/US

~~POST~~
9/11 (1973)

What would you know of
a feminism that stayed
up all night to track
an infant's breath? Re-
contact me when a child has
quickened the pulse of

YOUR BREADTH.

PETIT À PETIT

Metate y mano—like scansion, horizontal, but able to hold in the imagination History's vertical aspirations . . . Poco a poco. Nano a nano. Grind grief into the shadow. Of its former self: maiz(e). In a tortillería, someone almost convinced me that blue corn resists genetic modification. I'd like to believe that not everyone has her price. *Los* *pueblos originarios* come to mind. A friend queried, "¿Un mexicanismo?" "No, neologically speaking, the intellectual property of a broader constituency." *Spacetime* re- generates an Other's spine ("el otro lado"), by-the-by, the

In the middle of this culture of predicament, exhibit petit a: *the material object*

shabby angle of History's *why?*-access, coeval. *Un granito de arena . . .* Mano a mano—mete la mano—hand to hand. Sometimes repetitive action's a plan until the tool so becomes the Man, no *One* re-members sep/a/ra/tion's how-to. (Shuck the husk of the hold.)

FAMILY PORTRAIT (Wexner Center for the Arts, The Ohio State University, March 2007). I stand apart, daydreaming Technicolor, technicalities (the camera—my call to the arm's length). In deed, my shadow—like yours—bespeaks shades of gray, black, and white, the newly relineated afternoon's delight of what unites (and separates). Lin's *Groundswell* (1992–93)—Maya technology—deftly knells a landscape of the feminine, that barren plenitude of anticipation, which blinds the fruits' softest spots, the melancholy of what is not. *A Strong Clear Vision*. Bells ring murkier for me, a mercurial rise and fall, the indecision of spring, a springboard for revisiting Antigone's, *Will you share the labor, share the work?* Your father and I began, a broader politics of the question, *Will you help me have a child?* I cannot write about this now; something eruptive interrupted. In the bedroom, Ricardo Ruiz's *The Songs My Father Taught Me Are the Songs I Teach My Son* (1994) awaits, another landscape—a father and son extend a hand to a tree draped in lilac, pre-Pentecostal as Lent. Lent to my imagination (the pitfalls of allegorical overidentification), before you were born I sang a song, too, *I am the reluctant tree. Your father's the figure linking you to me. Why do you also hold the hand of death?* The question flush-flared a truce when I least expected it. *Through a glass darkly*, I witnessed the rush to gift rebirth—an artificial resurrection, petechiae, like flowers, blooming on your limbs. I watched three shades float-flee, cloak themselves in mourning, partake of a caretaking. Since then, that shadow economy, a second wind, kinship-diagrams the unfamiliar—our portrait, a groundswell of broken glass, asymmetrical as your legs' circumferences, a stark remainder of blockage, the paradox of the hourglass' torrential embargo.

"What Is the Difference between Globalization and Neoliberalism?"

~~Last week someone asked me,~~ "What is the difference between globalization and neoliberalism?" ~~The question isn't as innocent as it sounds. If all of us are imprecated in the cat-and-mouse game of cause and affect, who wouldn't apprehend the pair—at the bare minimum—as kissing cousins, as twin towers? Sure to go down, in historical terms, this is how the world turns: purgative reportage from Iraq serves as the perennial reality-check, presumptive as the corrective,~~ *Well, at least, I don't live in Fallujah.* Packing a one-two punch, purple-hearted Michigan slumps deeper into the driver's seat of depression. Aggressively passive, voters pass Proposition 2, designer-drug legislation with the intent to euthanize affirmative action (euphemized "The Civil Rights Initiative"), even as the state's Supreme Court rescinds queer Michiganders' bare-boned benefits. I wonder, *Where did I move?* A friend explains to me the intricacies of false advertising, *Here is the shape of the mitt, we're somewhere to the thumb's Left.* Directionally impaired, tone-deaf, I take cartography in like a fist. Stone-butch blues infuse the landscape with touching resistance. Industry, like a snow-bird, flexes its mobile muscles, ~~while, individuals (hermetically sealed) orchestrate equally market-driven *Jackie Brown* heists of citizenship.~~ I will grant you the once removed diehard few who stay put for museums' erections. ~~One for the auto, two for the Arab-American, three for the Motor City's revitalization (*Don't mourn, organize*).~~ In the hospital, I sit elongated hours with my son. A woman eyes us and no one in particular, *Is your kid Mexican?* ~~Calloused malice, like a flag at half-mast, hangs haggard as her expression when summoned. Six degrees of separation, peripheral as vision, somebody's piling it on: Once upon a time, it would have made a world of difference to partake of the blue pill instead of the red. Let's split the difference—civilization and its discontents, globalization/neoliberalism, the New World's Borderization. How schmaltzy to recycle the local's ashes when the transplanted's rejection looms, imminent as an organ. The chickens have come home to roost, environmentalism's ogres are loose, and we can only talk about the whether.~~ Or not. ~~Underground, centrifugal truth pacts a Faustian plot.~~ Lot's pillar salts and melts, but recasts its lot with the dammed—"new ethnicities" on the horizon ~~that slouch toward Bethlehem, terraforming interactive screens.~~ The night is young, middle age, a means to an end. Sipping creature comforts, pretend that the ~~performatively~~ tautological amends the conciliatory constellations of History, that the sciences of fiction stand on the shoulders of their own—two feet under. **If you follow this totemically taboo logic, even planets become subaltern subjects. Witness Pluto's recent downgrade.** ~~Now try to make an alternate case for the "Recline of the West."~~ Expect nothing less than a free Fall into the postscriptual.

"One need not be a Chamber—to be Haunted—"

I used to believe there is nothing more labor-intensive than cultivating a "jealous and suspicious mind." I'd prefer bone-weary work any day or night to the "weapons of the weak." Jealousy curves the spine, curls the penis and the toes' tips. It tips the scales, introduces a lisp, scalding the tongue and the roof of the mouth. ~~As soon as the door swings shut, I rifle through piles of books and papers, dresser drawers. I investigate the far recesses of closets and shelves, straining to amass the unmentionable.~~ A friend of mine described abjection: when her fiancé left for work, she would unearth his ex's blue jeans, bras, and panties that he kept tucked away (thinking her unaware). Each day she would forego breathing to fit into clothes two sizes too small, approaching her predecessor's lithe form as an impassable mountaintop. When the clothes mysteriously disappeared, she found herself distraught for weeks afterward, unable to account for the longing they'd been assigned. I have no designs on my spectral competition. ~~I don't know who she is; or, if, in fact, they (she in the plural) exist in the sepulcher beyond self-incrimination. I have had involuntary and unlimited access to my lover's checkered past (courtesy of those he's passed over "for greener pastures").~~ Ours was a spot-contract: I petitioned his assistance in having a child. No questions asked, no strings attached. The unexpected contemporaneously blossomed, but, was nipped in the bud: idealism's degeneration into the seedy underworld of Love. In the sweet hereafter, I disembowel the base root of what I'd come to call connection. It has nothing to do with pleasure's mechanics. ~~It isn't a silence of the lambs; our child was bleating inside me when my lover executed a series of decisions that interrupted the production of affect (fucking him now affords me no second wind). Yes, I am—out-of-touch—pardoning myself neither the offense of guilt-by-association, the Adamic bomb (*She made me do it!*), nor the defense of Biology's imperative, a nesting-impulse, a pheromonic mnemonic.~~ I gamble on the Symbolic, the wait of negating negation: *what if he is not not true?* ~~If the grammatical faux pas of that double-jointed Imaginary jars your sensibilities, contemplate the blockage it line-breaks in my conscience.~~ Dickinson ate the apple and lived to plant its seed, "The Brain has Corridors—surpassing/Material Place—" A nibbled pomegranate drains the half-empty glass, partial paralysis (quaint as the imperative, *Suspend that dialectic!*), demure as Armageddon deferred. Sometimes pop culture counsels, *Get up, Trinity, get up! Walk away, scoop the baby into the crook of your arm, wrestle the horizon into a more manageable picture frame*; but, the salt and pepper of my lover's complexion mirrors the tug of a parallel universe—forgiveness—the longest shortest distance between the Ego and the Id. A leap of fate? I want to be a chamber, made. For him? The conspiracy, known as the body, role-calls. In me? Finite infinities, unrefined sugars, the knife broken off, clean, obscure the severity of the womb.

PATERNITY SUITE

It has been brought to my attention that many have mistaken the aforementioned individual for my husband. For the record, he and I exchanged neither rings nor vows. We share a son; ~~and, in the hot-and-cold of the moment,~~ we have entertained the possibility of reinventing ourselves. On the first postpartum Father's Day, our baby nearly passed away. For a month, we waited in the hospital. There is an intimacy, hard-earned, watching a technological resurrection. A durational peace—maybe—although doubts surely remain, like the racket of a spin-cycle. I know too much. Under other circumstances, one of us would be fish-food. ~~Instead, I string myself up like beads, shoulda-coulda-woulda . . . a catchy refrain, catchy as a cold.~~ *Cold feet, warm heart.* Love's like a car that won't start, a traveler's snowy night in an airport parking lot. Baggage-and-baby's entourage, I press my nose against a copier's glass; I walk an arcade's unfinished project, envious of couples' spontaneous combustion. His embrace exudes a Platonism, *if not, winter,* then, its noir secrets, garbled as a space heater, insistent as a bagpipe. *Defrost*—rhythm equates loss with the awareness of absence, four echo chambers, made manifest in ~~regret's handshake, an iron-maiden's clasp, wistful as the forensic evidence of a Vestal Virgin's middle passage.~~ She's right—I stand on quicksand—unable to pass golden apple-laden boughs, or the rope, ripe for Hitchcock.

PILLOW TALK

after Tammy Rae Carland

How do you make a lesbian bed?
Leave the sheets crumpled
so she can come again.

THE ZÉ BAR

after Sadie Benning

Sleepy
lions,
Grrrr . . .
Elevators
that sing,
Bing!
It's dark now.
Let your
Chicago be
the night's
light.

ARRESTED DEVELOPMENT

~~Middle ages handle love with the sing-song candor of kid gloves so the mind can pick up mo' mementos. A story sticks in the craw:~~ an anthropologist fieldworking India found herself and her girlfriend caught in the act of making love. **Expecting swift retaliation, they were shocked by** the witness's interpretation—"two women minting money." **Cultural counter-fits? Absolution-by-informant? Realism's vertigo? These days, I also tread uncharted waters.** Coming of age lesbian, I mocked the monotony of the money-shot. Now it's as if I wear a T-shirt with the logo, HETERO, silkscreened across my chest. Sometimes it serves me right—airport security feels a might less frisky. But, at other times, the gilded cage of melancholy preordains my songbird's destiny. And, like the apple on William Tell's head, I am shot into a flowerbed, genealogy's perennial. This is the kiss of another spiderwoman's bliss: *Be careful what you wish for.* ~~A penny for your thoughts. I know not what I've done. Meanwhile, back at the split-level ranch, the gravity of the situation eludes elucidation. You got peanut butter in my chocolate! (Some Coke-laced-memento experiment, boy-meets-girl skin flick.)~~ Like cutting teeth, it's a re-release, *Don't bite the breast that feeds you.*

~~SIMULTANEOUS TRANSLATION~~

para Melissa McGill y Valentin Sabiote Ortiz

> *... lorsque le marbe porte et saisit à l'infini des plis qui ne s'expliquent plus par le corps, mais par une aventure spirituelle capable de l'embraser.* —Gilles Deleuze

El problema es que el pie está en el aire. If the toes are too small, they will break off. About face: ¿Entonces, podrías recortar los otros? The marble from here was not workable (although it trusted we'd reinvent ourselves . . .). ¿Cuánto tiempo llevas trabajando con mármol? ~~I belabour the negative space of the day's hollow.~~ This is the town that dusts itself. One hundred years. By accident we happened upon Las Canteras. And, the opening was in and unto a fold. Fold upon folds, the material, baroque. Cada escalera es de mármol; cada banqueta, una pizarra, contando, "Nunca les dejaré solos...." ~~The figures are meant to listen to the stone. Now I move toward the monumental. The snake of a road that unwinds the hill that pockets a watch to make time stand still . . . Macael, como si fuese un lugar, palpitando una poética prosa (quizás de Cortázar o García Márquez). Lo maravilloso real (about faith), a return—a portal, a window, a lesson, unlearned. I Schiavi (Dawn↔Dusk, Night↔Day) salen de la piedra, resistiendo La Entrada inevitable: "La escultura es la esencia del espíritu que toma forma, el grito de liberación en pugna con la materia..."~~ The line of a foot, the arch of a back, tickled into another format. <u>Nada en gris, por favor.</u> ~~Tell him I've waited to meet the work's match, tell him he's caught the impulse of the hand.~~ Confío en tu capacidad de traducir lo que me mueve hasta que me pliegue al réves. The stone, warm, slowly worn into smoothness, accelerates the pace of the chest's organ. The steady hum of machinery, quick to invent "(in)compossibility." *Just as the toes could level out, the sky breathes and thickens into itself . . .* ~~This marble is stronger than Carrara's.~~ Ni se envejece, ni se cansa como él de allá. Simultaneously mimetic, invective, current, translateably disproportionate: "*Pero hay los que luchan toda la vida...*" (like a leg grown longer than the day permits); *I usher myself into my opposite.*

HI-FI

Who hurt you, mamá?
God bless you!

Clumsy as a child is
graceful, too. He totters

in my footsteps,
tries to fill my shoes.
Yeats's stilt-stalker,

(1 . . .
2 . . .
3 . . .)

thrice-removed.

Because women in the upper stories
demand a face at the pain.

Because children demand a plan,
however plain, a Daddy-long-
legs to cobble their shoes,

stilted as the grammar
we're obliged to abuse.
"Barnacle goose," sea-

horses on high,

"processions that lack"
still catch my eye.

HI-FI 2

"Was it worthwhile to lay—
with infinite exertion . . . ?"

Rich as Adrienne
(naked as a jaybird),
"I feel like them up there:

Exposed, larger than life,
and due to break my neck."

The best laid plans
of micely men: women.

"Woe is me"—
the roof of my mouth,
a "burning deck"
of cards. I hold—close
to my chest, centrifugal as
a fugue—bested, interest,
"A life I didn't choose / chose me:"

(vested, recessive as a gene.)

FANNIE + FREDDIE

Ché ~~(Guevara©)~~: "You may have to be tough, but do not lose your tenderness. You may have to cut the flowers, but it will not stop the spring."

My dolce vita: "Let's have a salad instead."

$$\$\#@\%$$

Oh, those were the salad days!

Student loans handed out like government cheese.

No-money-down mortgages, flexible as arms, cuddly as kittens.

Like Sammy and Rosie, Fannie and Freddie got laid.

(Made in America®) *Off with their heads!* ~~Strikeover.~~

~~Strike out!~~ On your own. On with the parade.

The band played on.

"Bring it on." The red meat. The red whine.

As my mother says, "It's high time…"

Détroit: strait. Shot as the Midwest. Shot in the arm.

Middle passage—"MAE had a MAC."

There's more than one way to shock the patient ~~(line /~~

~~break)~~ reader . . . Hip huggers. Hit parade.

If you go down, I'll pre-pay.

"Gender or race, what'll it be? I don't have all day to set you free."

Let's apply ourselves, extend credit.

Tactfully tactical (mediated). ~~Unconscionable as the unconscious.~~

Let the hanger-oners have the honors.

"Ever felt like you're a missed opportunity?"

("This bud's for you."

"Lord, it's nippy.")

"Galvanized nipple?" I think in my head, "Tough titties! When my son's done with nursing, I'll have a jetset of those for the price-tag of one."

For the love-child of God!

For clothes!

For other flights of fancy that leave my lipstick smudged—

"That's no lady . . . !"

(Pitbulls and pigs. Domesticants?

Domestic: *Yes we can!*) Doubting as Thomas,

capital as Hill. Since when was politics a landfilled apologia?

"Forgive me for what I've done." For what? "I do." For what I'll become . . .

Open as a relationship.

Consolidated as "alone."

I rest my case on my laurels, but neither party pays the rent.

Alien ~~(alienated)~~ as Allen (Ginsberg, ~~not Woody~~): "When can I go into the supermarket and buy what I need with my good looks?"

Moon rising over Crooklyn. Let's balance the books

on other people's heads. And shoulders (above the rest).

Guaranteed as backstopping.

Now there's a war chest to stop your trafficking!

Necker-cubed, charter-schooled token of my affection—

you get what you pay for, you pay for what you get:

deficit spending, weaning prophets.

Here's the Real—*Deal?*

Make. Believe. Delegate.

Authorities: one in five families will go off the deep end.

Heaven help us . . .

Gerrymandered as Michigan.

Election-challengers, election-challenged.

Color—*dears*—blind? (a) blue≠red, (b) blue=red, (c) purple-hearted (type, set)

A bumper, cropped as the writing on the ~~wall~~ horizon:

Heaven helps those who help themselves . . .

Maybe the shattered ceiling isn't all it's cracked up to be.

"Coldest State, Hottest Governor."

Some Like it Hot.

Artsy, crafty as a bailout.

Blowback!

(*You gotta love that little blue dress from the Gap!*)

Too close to call.

Let's call it: ~~(Milton had a Friedman,~~

A Brief History of Neoliberalism) even.

A spayed's **a spade.**

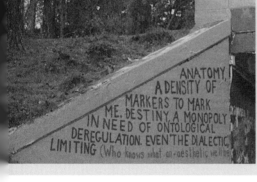

~~INTERROGATIVE~~

Heedless, soon headless, passerby / himself and herself—

~~How often did you commend each other's practices of deception (or, was the element of surprise so deep / so wide that you could not find the bullet's point of exit)?~~

~~Did she ask after the pregnant body's exhilarating need for speed—the arrogation of the whole, the scorched scent of descending sorrow—in the conversational quotidian?~~

~~Flowers, mourning (did she drink her coffee black or with cream? Did you bring it to her pillow talk of dreams?).~~

~~Shredding the sheets, did the two of you believe in once and future galaxies, the consolation of the constellations?~~

~~Did each of you wonder, *Is the other the One / the zero, indivisible as the lump sum of gravity?*~~

~~"An apple can fall up."~~
~~(You claim,~~

~~Did you also ride that trick-pony with her?~~

~~Did the shoe fit, did you wear it?~~

~~How frequently did you slip into something more comfortable?~~

me?
And,

~~Irrational as an integer, what did I wake-dream to replicate, to reconceive— myself—connective as tissue, soft as a fig, vulnerable as a hatchling?~~

~~A you (times two), sauntering?~~

~~Indexical indecision, rotating on the access of a thumb, the dubious honor of interrogation?~~

~~Heedless horseman—~~
~~Unable to be, come, clean as a clearinghouse, I choke, cherry the son, typecasting morality as abjection, as fetal forays into an enchanted forest of confectionary decathexis, as the sentinel mark of the Question.~~
~~As cyclical as finite, the solution: our shadows brush-burn—the non-Euclidean distance—I cannot put between our~~
~~ selves.~~

INTERNATIONAL WOMEN'S DAY 2007 Tonight, I've taken a solemn vow to allow national Women's Day 2007 happened to coincide with the poetic 'incident' I'm about to relate. poetics on a daily basis. Expect a pause, a hum, a click of connection and distance, the breath before touchy-feely to stem the tide of *pre-approval, a lower mortgage rate, protection against identity theft, a* and its anonymous speaker off-guard. *Please remove me from your call list.* I strive for a middle passage ~~Césaire. Eight weeks later he brushed up against the grain of death. His father and I stood on the~~ ~~when you're assigned a social worker, who communicates in hushed line breaks. I named my son~~ ~~sterile attitude of a spectator, for life is not a spectacle, a sea of miseries is not a proscenium, a man~~ ~~conceived of otherwise. Locating its impetus in the performativity of the quotidian, it eschews~~ all week for this reading; I dreamt of hearing *Crush* aloud. I cannot forget Césaire's emergence, poems until the breath's jagged edge became inseparable from the dictates of another performative convinces me that he recognizes the collection's soundtrack. The poet dramatically pauses, *I cannot* ~~public. The camera rolls, I bark, meek as a troll, *The stroller is over there*. As someone navigates my~~ ~~pleasantries of a Lefty bookstore evaporate. I was evicted from a summer sublet. I was dragged from an~~ ~~party. But, if this doesn't beat all!~~ I bite my tongue, I taste blood, swallowing impertinence, ~~How does~~ motherhood? Probably not. I told you I don't believe in that rhetorical trick-pony; but, maybe, this *unable to think?* The answer surfaces, precious as the line breaks—*the imposing silence after I click off baby's coo, but the war machine, inflexible as the seamy underside of a holier-than-thou poetics.* Somewhere as their cord-blood in the global North). Somewhere someone is practicing English in a mirror in year's wages to get her son's tongue clipped (for the purpose of English acquisition, ditto, in the I have an undying affection) might seem in the face of History's angel (hindsight is rootless), ~~when~~ ~~if it were the balancing act that it is.~~ Poised on San Diego's "poetry bridge," I find ~~that challenge~~ skeleton architecture of our lives. It lays the foundations for a future of change, a bridge across our ~~broken. It is something like imagining borders, which prove permeable enough themselves to~~ into contact with a poetic telemarketer? Once again, I'll cede the last word to Richard Siken, *was mine."*

myself to sound like Adrienne Rich, circa 1973 (*Diving Into the Wreck*). Keep this in mind: Inter-
We've come a long way, but not far enough NOT to have to reconstruct the parameters of our
a swimmer's plunge. If you catch on fast enough, go ahead and hang up. I'll concede I'm too
burial plot, a prescription drug plan . . . I listen for the second moment that breath will catch me
between compassionate fatigue and no nonsense. Eleven months ago, I gave birth to my son,
other side of the glass in an emergency room, watching the doctors intubate. You know it's bad
after the poet from Martinique, who forewarned mid-century, " . . . beware of assuming the
screaming is not a dancing bear . . . " Motherhood's engendered in me a poetics I could not have
epiphany, but favors interruption. *No telephone to heaven* unless *heaven rests beneath our feet.* I waited
emboldened as that collection's sepia sex. *Crush* accompanied me through labor and delivery. I spit
matrix. Cooing and humming as we duck into the bookstore's adjoining room, Césaire almost
think above the baby sounds. Silence, revolutionary as a guillotine, falls on the reading's illustrious
elbow, the pram's strong-armed out of the room. I muse, *No time for niceties, coats and hats, the*
auditorium in the service of civil disobedience. Dirty dancing got me a one-way ticket out of a
it feel to be a literary bouncer? Is this my mini-epiphany regarding an ethics of listening, a poetics of
has something to do with the sea-cum we are all swimming through. I ask myself, *What leaves you*
the radio, the computer, the television, after I am force-fed a barrage of reported carnage. Not the sounds of a
someone is repeating the maxim, *Children should be seen, not heard* (or, better yet, unseen, banked
the hopes of becoming a telemarketer in the global South. Somewhere someone is paying a
global South). I told you I'd sound like Adrienne Rich! But, cheesy as 1970s feminism (for which
Césaire came to, after the respirator was removed, I double-dog dared myself to live each day as
echoed in Audre Lorde's structural benediction, "Poetry is not only dream and vision; it is the
fears of what has never been before." Imagine a line that actively resists the conceit of being
permit greater migrations, rescripting continents. Have you ever had the dubious pleasure of coming
"What would you like? I'd like my money's worth. . . . *Sorry about the blood in your mouth. I wish it*

33

SIGN AGE SIGNAGE
process note for *Economy of Gesture*
(San Diego/Tijuana, 2008)

Sign spinning is regionally inflected. If San Diego sign spinners are predominately young male tricksters, guilded in the tricks of their trade, Ann Arbor/Detroit/Ypsilanti sign spinners embody the middle-aged down-and-out. Put differently, as a general rule, San Diego spinners exude style, promoting their expert moves as well as businesses and goods in the nearby vicinity; whereas, spinning Michiganders appear more akin to placeholders, outposts amidst the elements, withstanding subprime mortgages and temperatures.

Two hauntings: in frigid December, a forty-something woman stands, toddler in tow, at a busy intersection upholding a sign, which ironically reads, "Come in out of the cold with a $3.99 pizza." Her face is implacable, resigned. My mind imagines "situations," what brings a lone mother to the position of being a human directional in inclement weather—layoffs, foreclosures, unemployment that foreshadow a nationwide recession, the contagious pathos of the Rustbelt. (If corporations are people too, do they dream of blue skies ahead?) In March, "under the perfect sun," an unshorn Statue of Liberty performs a lackluster spinning, barely able to lift his advertisement for help with taxes. This dragging queen's circumstantial evidence seems as striking as the Michigan spinner's—an almost anomaly, a slip of the slip, profound as that of Lady Liberty's crown-of-thorns on his disheveled head.

Initially unaware of the deregulated elements of spinning, I perceived spinners to be quaint anachronisms, holdovers from a pre-digital era in which advertisers paraded as sandwiches for pittance and cultural penance—personifying the disposability of the worker and the advert. More recently, my mind layers, I see double—the picket line's placard (another anachronism, or, so we're sold), the walkout, the strike's mockery, labor's "animated suspension" (no suspended dialectic, but proof-positive of the incorporation of the legend of "the Left").

(Performance) artist Sharon Hayes explains her series of one-woman interventions as contrasting allegory and anachronism. Hayes creates solitary protest, recycling poster slogans from the past ("Who Approved THE WAR IN—Vietnam?," "I AM A MAN," "Ratify E.R.A. NOW!") to place them out-of-context. Puncturing, punctuating publics like soap bubbles, she stands alone at street corners, on the steps of courthouses. Anachronistic? I suppose, but, perhaps more allegorical of the Derridean slippage between anachronism and anarchy.

I know sign spinners earn their living/s. But, I'm inclined to read their mirroring affect (their economy of gesture/gesture of economy) as allegorical fragments of the political unconscious, as the signs and signage of a Sign Age in which there's cognitive dissonance between the message ("Come in out of the cold," "Liberty Taxes") and the messenger-becoming-meta-message (the freezing Mother-Child dyad, the citizen-turned-spinning-statue–key performance indicators of the ways and means by which liberty *taxes*).

RVICE TE	CPT CODE	DESCRIPTION		AMOUNT

POST/PAR/TUM/DOC/U/MENT
after Mary Kelly

Date	Code	Description	Detail	Amount
/21/06		MEDEX SYRINGE PUMP		111.00
/21/06		MEDEX SYRINGE PUMP		111.00
/21/06	80048	LAB-METABOLIC PANEL BASIC IP		91.00
/21/06	83735	LAB-MAGNESIUM		43.00
/21/06	84100	LAB-PHOSPHORUS		25.00
/21/06	85007	LAB-DIFFERENTIAL MANUAL IP		33.00
/21/06	85025	LAB-CBC W/PLTS & DIFF IP		47.00
/21/06	87040	LAB-CULTURE BLOOD IP		110.00
/18/06	87184	LAB-ANTIBIOTIC SENSI,KB IP		99.00
/21/06	87088	LAB-CULTURE URINE IP		88.00
/21/06	J0460	ATROPINE 0.1 MG/ML 10ML SYR	ATROPINE 0.1MG/ML SY	12.51-
/21/06		ROCURONIUM BROMIDE 10MG/ML	ROCURONIUM 10MG/ML V	35.63-
/21/06		KETAMINE HCL 10MG/20ML INJ	KETAMINE HCL 10MG/ML	11.23-
/23/06		PRIVATE		1155.00
/22/06	97003GO	OT-INITIAL EVAL, EA 15 MINS	(QTY OF 0002)	126.00
/22/06		RESUSCITATION BAG,PER DAY		47.00
/22/06	94762	PULSE OX; CONTINUOUS MONITOR		273.00
/22/06		DRESSING CHANGE		71.00
/21/06		SUTURE, A KUHLMAN	(QTY OF 0002)	12.00
/21/06		NEEDLE PERC 21G 1"-ARGON		39.00
/21/06	C1893	SHEATH 4.5F PICC TEARAWAY-BRAU	(QTY OF 0002)	170.00
/21/06	J2250	MIDAZOLAM PER 1MG INJ	(QTY OF 0002)	40.00
/21/06	C1769	GUIDEWIRE .018" COPE-COOK		77.00
/21/06	C1769	MICROPUNCTUR KIT 4CM COPE WIRE		58.00
/21/06	J2270	MORPHINE SULF,UP TO 10MG INJ		14.00
/21/06		LIDOCAINE 0.5% 50ML INJ		8.00
/21/06	99145	MOD SED EA ADT'L 15MINS	(QTY OF 0003)	90.00
/21/06	99143	MOD SED <5YRS 30MINS		200.00
/21/06	36568	TR-INSERT PICC W/O PRT/PUMP <5		877.00
/21/06	J1644	HEPARIN SODIUM, 1000 UNITS		1.00
/22/06		IV SOLUTION-COMMERCIAL	DEXTROSE 5%-1/4NS IV	41.00
/22/06		VITAMIN A & D 60GM OINT	VITAMIN A & D OINTME	11.58
/22/06	J1650	ENOXAPARIN INJ 10MG	ENOXAPARIN 10MG/ML *	16.47
/22/06		NONFORMULARY EXTEMP INJ	AMPICILLIN 30MG/ML I	20.02
/22/06		NONFORMULARY EXTEMP INJ	AMPICILLIN 30MG/ML I	20.02
/23/06		NONFORMULARY EXTEMP INJ	AMPICILLIN 30MG/ML I	20.02
/23/06		NONFORMULARY EXTEMP INJ	AMPICILLIN 30MG/ML I	20.02
/22/06		DUAL INF PUMP-SIGNATURE GOLD		94.00
/22/06		MEDEX SYRINGE PUMP		111.00
/22/06		MEDEX SYRINGE PUMP		111.00
/24/06		PRIVATE		1155.00
/21/06	93971	DUP SC EXT VEINS UNIL-UE OR LE		398.00
/24/06		IV SOLUTION-COMMERCIAL	DEXTROSE 5%-1/4NS IV	41.00
/23/06		NYSTATIN/TMC/WWB/MOM	RASH CREAM - UMH	24.00

August 29, 2007

XXXX Carmel St.
Ann Arbor, Michigan XXXXX
Landline: 734-xxx-xxxx
Cell: 919-xxx-xxxx
Email: xxxxxx@umich.edu

Medical Records
University of Michigan Hospitals
2901 Hubbard
Suite 2722B
Ann Arbor, Michigan 48109

To Whom It May Concern:

Please release **ALL** of the medical records, including and especially dopplers and MRIs, of my sixteen-month-old son, Césaire Jose Carroll-Dominguez (birthdate: 4/21/2006, registration #: xxxxxxx25) to the following address:

Prof. Dr. med. Xxxxx Xxxxx-Xxxxx
Klinik und Poliklinik für Kinderheilkunde
-Pädiatrische Hämatologie/Onkologie-
Albert-Schweitzer-Str. 33
D-48149 Münster, GERMANY

Tel: +49-(0)xxx-xx-xxxxx
Fax: +49-(0)xxx-xx-xxxxx
Email: xxxxxx@uni-muenster.de

Césaire has a scheduled appointment with Prof. Dr. med. Xxxxxx Xxxxx-Xxxxx on October 15, 2007. The doctor has requested that these records arrive no later than two weeks prior to the appointment. Please do not hesitate to contact me if you have any questions.

Many thanks,

[signature: Amy Sara Carroll]

Amy Sara Carroll

AN ANTI-FOUNDATIONAL FOUNDATION
EXTRA-TERRESTRIAL COMMUNICATION

...grew more loathsome until one morning a funny thing happened. Despite all contraindications, you chose to inhabit me. No bigger than the size of a flea, a fetus on record to give the ultrasound technicians and your mother the peace sign. Peace mom, peace mon. Little in utero activist who renders his mother ticklish after her many years of disavowal, left me with the sensation that once can be made discoverer of new ways to move. I said to your father, I need to nap, I need a nap sit down. But, he and I are not the most amiable four-legged. Adept at fitting in, we sit, but telling is stark, rigid as an adolescent, I finger the remembrance of your playful somersaults—a series of grainy photographs—my own mother comments on your strong jaw. Meanwhile, I recall the story of a friend, watching her nephews from her office window even as she's forbidden to see them face-to-face. I muse, May I eschew prohibition and welcome you and all who together contain open arms, a phrase I repeat as I sit on the toilet, dizzy of organizational lapses, for my wandering I, for the doubts I harbor, yes, carry inside. Beside you? Perhaps, but somehow I imagine your compartment in the story I imagine. We are weaving for you a gray cocoon, a swing out of the gossamer threads of our fluid and intoxicating affections, small light with Hurricane Katrina victims, insisting. If you and jellybean were hungry, I would break into houses. I laugh inside (you must feel the jiggle), thinking aloud (well, in the mind's eye). If jellybean and I were hungry, if you were hungry and strong and free to love the men and women with whom you'd come in contact. May you savor and bask, eyes closed and cheeks with the bend of a honeybee's may knock twice if you can hear this, three times if you'd like to hear more. May you dwell in peace, but forgive yourself which darkness creeps into the hollow of your heart. May you dwell in between yes and no, in the pocket of the hour and its iridescent shadow. A time machine, a slow-release capsule, dodging the cartographers and their grafts to refute quantifiable cause and affect, may you—in the close quarters of collaboration—map "a world in which many worlds fit."

CAT CARRIER

LANUGO

In Fallujah, U.S. troops are using white phosphorous in combat situations. White phosphorous burns the skin to the bone. Sometimes actions can have similar effects even if their manifestations are not immediately apparent on the body. Your father wants to be with me for your birth. This isn't a sign like the double rainbow I saw when I was on the way to get tested to assess whether you were and are "chromosomally sound." It isn't a sign like the three dolphins arcing out of the water, which I witnessed on a ferry boat ride back from Ocracoke the weekend after my graduation.

The other passengers had congregated at the back of the boat, I meandered my way to the front and again began to think about all I had done and all I had not. I grew melancholic, *If only life would offer up a sign that things will be okay.* Three dolphins appeared as if in response, I blinked and they were gone, and I thought, *No, that didn't happen,* until suddenly they broke the water again. In contrast, I'm pretty sure your father's going to leave us when the novelty of the situation wears off. Still, it's nice of him to stick around for a little awhile—which doesn't mean his attentions haven't confounded me in the last few months, mainly because he's implicitly and explicitly contrasted them with his overarching love life confusion that amounts to his relationships with at least two women, XXXX and XXXXX. I didn't know much about the pair, but when he did tell me the details of his double-yoked involvement with them, I wasn't really bothered by the situation until he began to profess an interest in us. I guess I thought he didn't want to be anything more than a sperm donor so his newfound desire to be an important part of both of our lives initially rang disingenuous to me.

But, my feelings for your father are nothing if not complicated. The overarching sensation I have for him is one of abiding love. Perhaps it is what prompted me to ask for his help in this collaboration. What I didn't know is that he also harbored a deep desire to have a child. Now I sense that he confuses that desire with an affection for me. I try not to take his attentions personally, to keep the two things separate because I am determined not to fall in love with him. My insistence is hard to explain in terms that do not smack of melodrama. It's just that it isn't the kind of love I want anymore. I am longing for something steady and constant. Unfortunately, though, spinning the straw of this confession into gold, *I know that a part of me already fell in love with him long ago.* This past month I have listened to him agonize over his two relationships. In turn, I have negotiated his attempts to hijack my dreams, his insistent insertion in my narrative fantasy of long-term commitment. One night he said he wanted to be my "boyfriend," I didn't respond.

I thought, *It's finally sinking in that I'm pregnant and alone in the process. First, I transferred my emotional energies to your father in subtle ways. Recently I've begun to realize that his acts of transference outstrip mine; but, I can't really carry this along with you, so I am going to have to let him and his emotional weather storms exit my radar screen.* I resist calling him the evening before his trip to New York City. I long to hear his voice, but earlier that afternoon when I returned his phone call, he was a study in distance, saying we would talk later when he had a chance. *Lay Ter?* I think, *we need to promise each other nothing more than Arundhati Roy's "tomorrow." When the stakes get higher, we both panic and pull away despite the intimate in-between we're coming to know as our child.*

These days I happen upon the wish that I had not chosen an alternative route for shepherding you into the world. Uncertainty brands me when what I want to know is your quickening movements in utero. There are so many ways to be lonely and I've perfected several in my lifetime. Unfortunately, I have a hunch I will expand my repertoire. But, maybe with a bit of luck, I will meet someone to share some of the journey. That person is not your father; he is a makeshift friend, but our visions of the future are a forked road and tongue. You are what we hold in common. On his return back from NYC, from his visit to his not so ex, he sings a rainy day tune—no mention of affections for me, but a blunt *I want to continue the relationship with XXXXX* in passing conversation regarding her indecision. I feel an instant burning to the bone; he continues, *I can't talk because I'm in a middle seat.* I envision passengers on either side of him internally shaking their heads, wishing for me a better situation. I am wishing that for myself. Indeed, this November morning, I feel like a cat carrier, like a kitchen appliance that happens to have a rabble-rousing fetus inside her, the convenient handmaiden who does not abort, but allows herself to grow large as a whale. And, following that shoestring flight of self-pity, I no longer simply cry myself to sleep or wake up sobbing; the quotidian also betrays the tracks of my tears in ways that glow more cumbersome by the hour.

39

CORRESPONDENCE
20/20

After twenty weeks I have received emails from your father's lovers. They present themselves as evacuation women who never achieve an orgasm, women who were never a lover at all. Their anger perplexes and saddens me. I hate them. The doctor pronounces you "perfect"—examining the three-soon-to-be-four chambers crumple like tissue paper as I read their diatribes against the three of us. Their accusations ring like of your heart, an area in the back of your brain, the train of your spine, your tiny fists uncurlcurses brought down upon your head. I cannot resist imagining them as wicked witch characters, ing to reveal ten fingers, your feet replete with their ten toes, your stomach, your mouth, I always loved). It's difficult because their vitriolic missives attack not only me or him, but you as your eyes behind their lids. I marvel at what we witness—your tiny profile, your face peering well. In response, I feel a groundswell of emotion—is this "maternal instinct"? I want to protect you back, the certainty of your sex (a distinct pillar that renders the ultrasound "pornographic" in from their narrow readings of your conception and identity. I want to explain to you that I never the words of your grandmother), your lovely recline which includes a cat stretch. knew the extent of your father's attachments to these letter-writers. I asked him *as a friend* to Your father is silent beside me, more contemplative in his processing of your presence. I am me bring you into this world. Approaching his presence as a matter of possession, they bemoan the reminded of the first time I saw you at twelve weeks when the news did not seem as good. loss of someone precious, implying that I snatched him away in some intricate plot

Days later, after more invasive testing, I went to a sesquicentennial celebration of the publicaIt's odd, I resist asking your father for any form of commitment; and, believe it or not, my hunch retion of Walt Whitman's *Leaves of Grass*. Those of us in attendance formed a circle and took turns mains to maintain a critical distance from the boxing ring. Even when your father suggests different reading the poem aloud. I'd never heard it in one sitting with so many different voices contribconfigurations for our relationship, I have serious doubts that the two of us have any future like the uting to the melodious cacophony that already abounds. I felt Whitman's tongue lap over us, one he or his ex's imagine. Instead, I hope for the best in a romantic friendship that has been like even as one line in particular stood out (a sentiment that had been lost on me previously in the nothing I've navigated previously. I harbor the conviction that he and I can nurture a collaboration midst of the volume's luscious linguistic reshuffling). *I know I have the best of time and space—and* built upon a deep-ceded ambition to be parents—NOT lovers—but parents of another human be*that I was never measured, and never will be measured.* ing. Consequently, when I open their attachments, I recognize neither myself nor him; but, wonder, Because pregnancy has accentuated my already melodramatic tendencies, I felt an overwhelmat the parameters of his past lovers' imaginations—that they view my pregnancy in such didactic, ing sorrow. *My son will never be able to write that*. And, following quickly on its heels, an impossible dyad-tinted terms. It's as if these women assume I aspired to board Noah's ark two-by-two to set *promise. Perhaps all this testing*—meant to reassure—*overlooks the obvious,"the best of time and space,"* sail into the sunset. *Silly rabbits, tricks are for kids*—when I think of the days ahead, one and one does *which all of us carry inside. My son may not be able to write the above, but he will never be measured* not equal three, and, it's you and I puddling through what's to come—mother and son—despite the *again.* A silly vow—like rules or fine china—meant to be broken, I hold it like a firefly mistakes I've committed. And, if correspondences exist between the visions of who I am projected cupped, illuminating the crawlspace of "radiant darkness" my body generates for your own. to be and who I actually am—the folds of uncertainty—the thighs' creases, the backs of the knees—that which fuels a quickening, petty reason, a belly to move.

PANICKING

> *It's my happening and it freaks me out!*
> Z-man, *Beyond the Valley of the Dolls*

Overbred as a toy poodle, I ask, "Is happiness hard-earned?" Then, I hit auto-reply, "I have taken the most meandering paths in pursuit of dreams, carefully testing and re-testing each step. Sometimes I have become exasperated with the circuitry of these routes. Still, I wish for you the ability to pursue your own dreams at your own pace, regardless of the dictates of those on the sidelines (including me, my little love, may there be times when you do NOT listen to my warnings, admonitions, or worse yet, unsolicited advice.)"

Winter is a difficult season for me—the snow and ice. I longed to escape Chicago's cold. The holidays in South Texas have not panned out to be what I expected—several days now with a head cold, long nights of drowning in little sleep, and yesterday evening spots of blood as I went to the bathroom. I panicked, thinking I was losing you. I tried to take a deep breath, but my lungs wouldn't cooperate. I called the doctor. He said perhaps I'd broken a cervical capillary coughing. If there weren't any contractions or further bleeding that I should rest for the next day and try to remain relaxed. That's easier said than done—each day I grow more attached to you as if the nutrients and oxygen that the umbilical cord provides flowed in both directions.

My lungs are my Achilles heel. I worry they will be your downfall, too. I haven't felt up to the task of protecting you in the last few weeks. I imagine an airplane flight. The stewardess advises, "Put the oxygen mask on yourself before attempting to help small children." I am fumbling with the cords and elastic band. I have never been good at mechanical tasks. I vacillate between following directions and choosing to aid you before myself. I want to call your father and ask if he also will pledge to protect you. Like most impulses, this one is irrational, linked to the sensation that I am not happy with my life right now. I'm particularly disturbed by the numbness and paradoxical lack of interiority into which I have fallen. Your father reports experiencing an intense happiness. In contrast, I feel duped, drugged, dumbed down, a bungling cow (like Sylvia Plath's images of maternity). Last night when I began to bleed, I said to myself, "This is only a dream, one that follows the theme of things not working out." I fingered the edges of other clichés, "how fragile we are in the face of improbability, how fragile, how strong, as human beings, awash in histories' jet-streams." Chart the progress of their flows. I start toying with my own affections, contemplating the prospect of failing you whether or not you choose to remain with me.

DREAMTIME

This is not a dream: I am standing in the kitchen. Your grandmother goes to take a knife out of its hanging wooden holder so that I can cut morning grapefruit. The holder crashes down on a glass, which shatters all over my face and body. I am ambered as an insect, caught between waking and sleeping. No one gets up to help. I try to steer myself into the bathroom. I wait outside the door for awhile as your aunt washes her face, puts in her contacts. I am shivering—not because I am cold, but because I don't know if anyone would support me if I got into real trouble. Minor lacerations are treated by my family as if they were variations on a theme or wish list. Indulgent in abjection, I think, *I would fret over any of them if this happened, pregnancy aside.* But, sometimes people are so clumsy in their caregiving that they stun those within their immediate orbits.

Like a small child, I counted the days until my Christmas holiday. Now I count the holiday hours that remain. I am sinking into a deep, hibernating depression. Winters in Chicago are brutal and the fall quarter was difficult enough. Your other aunt projects an aura—it is like cocoa, a bitterness, but I see it in terms of refraction. Pregnancy was not what I expected, but it has endowed me with extrasensory perception. Smells overwhelm; colors beckon or retract; touch is Whitman's "body electric"; sound amplifies itself into thin interwoven thread-like transmissions of pleasure and pain. But, sight, unsightly, dims it seems—objects blur around their edges so that even with glasses I tend to squint—except in the realm of affect. Now people carry auras, halos; as if I could read infrared, I feel myself perceiving emotion, forcefields of energy that reflect bone-chilling heat or down-comforter warmth (or gradations of that either-or). It's something like seeing red where red was the color I could not stomach in our first trimester.

This morning I crawl back into bed and contemplate time as a spool undone. I think, *I am out-of-joint, perennially nursing the adolescent sensation that I am shipwrecked on an apocalyptic island.* I brush a dream like a bead of sweat off my forehead: you are nursing, I shift you from one nipple to the other. You latch on, weak with hunger, but strong. I feel your tug as an affection I previously could not decipher. Then, someone poses the smirking question, *But won't you be unhappy in Ann Arbor without the sun?* My reply is comparable, an upside-down pun, *But I always will have my son when the afternoons decide to cut themselves short on nightfall.*

INTROJECTION

There is a thin, but durable, membrane between me and your father. I have built it in order to protect us. To protect whom? Me. You. Perhaps even him. I am afraid he will disappoint me to the extent that I will not be able to breathe, to go on in his company. I know that such a thing cannot happen; you will need me as much as you need me so I am determined to maintain an affective distance as a barrier against his deceptions. I scan his face, his voice, for telltale signs of intuitive counter-intelligence, some inkling or knowledge that I should make a clean break. I do not see anything to indicate that he is a "bad man" (as if I believe in that classification). Sometimes I encounter a kind of fatigue in fear of failure that mirrors my own. I think *I have no expectations. He has or will betray me* in some critical moment, so I will always have to protect you and myself against that inevitability. In deed and theory, I carry a parodic fatalism. He cannot be more than the sum of his past and future actions. And, with such an inverted calculus (Benjamin's angel sandblasted away from the rubbish of History), the guide, an attacked against him and we are taken along for the ride. Or maybe the story does a belly-flip. I hope not. I will betray him because for the first time in my life and I no longer trust him, and the consequences of that reversal of fortune have not caught up with us. Because I do not foresee the possibilities of osmosis, I wake up breathless each night since XXXX's email, an introjection I cannot afford to embrace and/or to lose. The dream proceeds as follows: I am crossing a chasm or leaning between tall buildings. He extends his hand. I place my trust in him. Then, suddenly, he withdraws that support and I plummet toward an uncertain future, cleaving along the fault line. I must cushion my fall so you will survive to tell the tale, to even eat the master at the table.

42

"I am an anachronism."

Like adolescence, pregnancy spawns in me ambitiously amphibious dreams, which juggle with their webbed feet the intricate details of the quotidian. I went to a conference at the School of the Art Institute of Chicago on "re-doing performance." Several artists presented, including Sharon Hayes, who contrasted allegory and anachronism. Hayes creates solitary protest, recycling poster slogans from the past ("Who approved THE WAR IN Vietnam?," "I AM A MAN," "Ratify E.R.A. NOW!") to place them out-of-context. She stands alone at street corners, on the steps of courthouses, presenting herself as a series of one-woman interventions. Anachronistic I suppose, but, perhaps more allegorical of the Derridean slippage between anachronism and anarchy.

The field of dreams: on the third anniversary of the war in Iraq, I join thousands in downtown Chicago to demand a rethinking of U.S. policy. I am a very pregnant woman amid a sea of marching people being reined in by police in full riot gear. Their presence follows me into sleep. I frighten myself into believing a stranger is in the apartment. Drifting in and out of dreams, frantic and breathless, I lock myself in the bedroom, scanning the neighborhood. The windows are sealed shut, I am watching policemen in perfect formation below. I know they are trained to shoot to kill. But, I also calculate I have only a slim month-and-a-half to attach onto the front of the apartment a platform-like porch that will allow you to escape. I scrawl in magic marker on a piece of poster board, "I am an anachronism."

I press it to the pain of glass, I hear the bedroom door rattle and wake myself up, sobbing like a queen-of-hearts, "Is this the anarchy of being born into the wrong era?" I remember adolescence as a time in which I felt I had arrived too late. While I romanticized the chaos of the 1960s, my peers seemed wholly uninterested in the political. Cynically, I might say I've inhabited inaction in the face of my own cynicism. Your father, in contrast, a bit ahead of me in the universe's plans, generates other ways and means. I know it is partly what draws and binds me to him— an intense admiration for his ability to believe in the direct action of literal and data-bodies. If I could I would beseech him to bequeath to you his unflinching optimism, the springtide in his step that circumvents the gravity of Lilliputians.

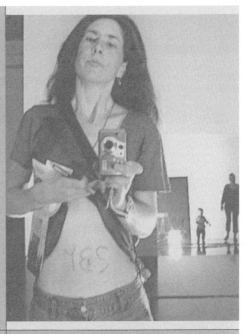

FALSE COGNATES

This morning your father asks me about your name. XXXXXXX XXXX XXXXXXX-? XXXXXXX XXXX XXXXXXX-YYYYYYYY? I have been thinking about that hyphenated difference for some time. The dustcloud of anxieties I associate with your naming revolves around the question of your father's presence: will he be there for you in two, five, ten years or will you be left with the ghost of a name? (I know I am not leaving.) I semi-quell the parallel, perennial anxieties I generate about my own relationship with your father by recognizing "he and I" as contingent, uncertain, dubious (a form of downplaying his importance to me). I wonder about the forces which pull us toward each other and about the counter-forces that compel us to push one another away. Reflected recently in our patterns of sleeping, this give-and-take bears repeating: where previously we kept to distinct sides of the bed, now, often, we curl into each other, cuddling my March middle. Like a rotisserie chicken, I turn and turn as if to brown you evenly. Your father accommodates such uneasy rest, realigning himself in relation to my belly's unruly dictates. Yet, once in our first or second trimester, he told me about a television program, which chronicled animals' parenting decisions. It seems in the realm of the nonhuman, a mother is called upon to recognize the distinction between a biological parent, the male creature who has helped her to become pregnant, and the parent, who eventually might aid her in raising her offspring. That "parable of the real" has burrowed into me; honestly, I don't know if he will be both parents to you. The steady tug of gravity may render such a fairy tale obsolete insofar as it remains quasi-dependent upon his and my relationship. Put differently, I wonder if "he and I" shines forth resplendently as a false cognate? "He and I": a phrase that would seem to harbor some obvious translation into another language— friendship, love— but, in reality bears no resemblance to what it sounds like? "He and I": a dyad best left to the "road not taken"? Maybe time will tell, but maybe time is tight-lipped, refusing to give any of its blood-thirsty plots away. And, XXXXXXX XXXX XXXXXXX-YYYYYYYY? Will your name showcase the traces of the father he could not be, revelatory of another false cognate? Or, will the weight of my insecurities snap your name's hyphen like a twig, like a wishbone, that, drying on the windowsill, sat for weeks, unattended? Here's a wish sure to wind: may he and I have the wisdom to separate our relationship from our relationships with you.

GRANDMA GRACULA
ON THE ANNIVERSARY OF HER DEATH

I am beginning my eighth month of pregnancy. You ride low or I carry you that way. So considerate, you do not interfere with my breathing. In the mornings, my breasts leak a thick yellow substance and then a translucent, watery white liquid, flavorless, but with a sweet aftertaste your father enjoys sampling. He is flying to New York City today to spend the weekend with one of his ex-s. I've given up trying not to be jealous or to sidestep this sadness inhabiting me. I wish he and I were different people. Even if he were to tell me that nothing would or did happen between his former lover and himself, I would not believe him; so, we've arrived at the impasse that I would prefer he simply not call versus check-in pretending that he misses you and me. I shouldn't answer the phone, but like a tack to a magnet, I am pulled to his voice with a morbid curiosity. Do I love him? Maybe I could if he would let me, but his behavior pushes me away, demarcating a clear distance between us. I obsess about "the god of small things": shoes for you, a stroller, a glider for nursing. I dream of XXXXXX, she is my age and we sit in her apartment, she watches my belly as if it might disappear at any moment. Then, she writes a number on a scrap of paper she pushes into my palm, "Call if you have any questions, if any emergencies arise and you are not up to the occasion." I think, "I never am."

At night, you decide to make your presence known. I wonder if you will take after your paternal grandmother, Graciela, who was inadvertently nicknamed by a careless journal's mailing label, "Gracula." She worked the graveyard shift as a lab technician (never the pathologist she could have been if she'd remained in Mexico). Her occupation facilitated your father's playful childhood conclusion that she must be a vampire. She, too, visits me in dreams. In December, she came to my bedside to introduce herself and muse, "He will fail you at crucial junctures, but I will do my best to help you with this child's transition into the world." I think you have many guardian angels, they hover at the bed's four posts (picture perfect as Juan Soriano's *Cuatro esquinitos tiene mi cama*) perhaps sufficient to protect you from the unknown, perhaps as ill-prepared as I feel in the face of deception and subterfuge.

Dear Illinois Mother:

BEFORE AND AFTER
THE BIRTHING PLAN FOR CÉSAIRE JOSÉ (OTHERWISE KNOWN AS ZÉ)
ENTRE COMILLAS

Pain

There is a quality to being pregnant that seems unreal to me, even as I recognize that sensation as cliched. I know that my life will be changed irrevocably after you are born, that I will never be the person I was, that always I will feel the break of "Before XX's birth" and "After." One winter afternoon, I saw the Grand Canyon for the first time. I could not get over that landmark's magnificence, the feeling that it wasn't quite real, that instead I must be in a well-disguised I-max theater. Pregnancy instills a similar sentiment of disbelief in me. Your tiny kicks, your insistent fists still astound my heart and my head. And, lacking an alternative explanation for their source, I imagine being inhabited by an alien. The doctor describes you as "the perfect parasite," taking from me whatever you like so that you can grow at an unspeakable clip, which, under any other circumstances, would cause an organism to implode. I know your lungs are almost ready now, that, if push came to shove, you could survive outside of my uterus, without me. But, my body does not take seriously the idea of your possible independence. Instead I wake each morning to leakage, my breasts secreting food for thought, my mind brushing off the grainy sands of sleep, registering your insistent movement (as if you were enjoining me to roll over, rearrange the pillows and sheets, or sing some impromptu tune). Yesterday my mother and I bought you a crib. A few weeks earlier we purchased a stroller. Slowly, I feel myself growing into some accommodation of adulthood, calling pediatricians and daycare providers, plotting out our lives in Ann Arbor after we leave the cocoon of Evanston. You will be my travelling companion, my partial manifestation of the rapid changes that will alter my own organism. Your father in response to such "before and after" clichés suggests "things won't really be that different, in fact, they might remain the same." I am and am not astonished that he can entertain such a fantasy of steady-state consciousness for himself. I know you will rewrite, reroute, reinvent, and round out the person I am, could be, and will become. "I'm ready," I think in the awareness that one can never be completely set for the high winds of utter transformation.

[Handwritten overlay:]

Congratulations on the new addition to your family! The arrival of your new daughter directly affects you and your family's future, but also that directly affects you and everyone's right to free, safe, healthy, and happy life — every woman's right to free, safe, her child. No matter, the place, public or private, discrimination is not only wrong, it is now illegal.

Again, congratulations.

Sincerely,

Patricia Blagojevich
Patricia Blagojevich
First Lady

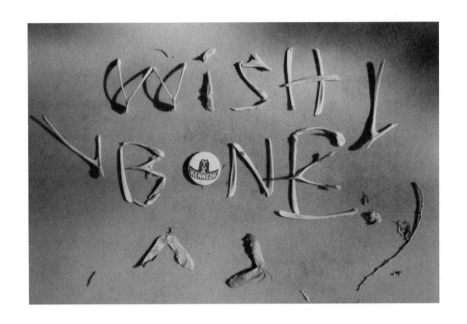

Coo.
Baby-
coup.

LET DOWN

I hang on the thread of a letter to you. Each day I resolve to include a snapshot of your wonder, but here it is going on a month and I've barely tucked away a moment to put my fingers to the keyboard. One month—you seem regal as the self-assured. A bellybutton all your own. A full head of hair and little nose freckled with acne. The luck of tummy gas to alter the course of what will pass from either end of the self. You pet me as you incessantly snack, I feel each micro-caress in contrast to the spinning of the breast's thread—that is the sensation—you're pulling a thread out of me in the process of a feeding, a persistent unraveling of some *hilo negro*. I grow equally desirous of your latch where more than two hours becomes a weight on the chest that commands relief in its excess. Your cry and I am letting down—the milk's weeping or shooting in a white-blue stream, the slightly turned smell of sweetness on your chin, dribbling off the sphere of the breast, your head lulling into my lap, then on my knees, we hear the blast of a burp as loud as a coal mine's collapse—today the world is caving in, I prop it up with toothpicks, the curl of your first smile.

INDUCTION
NOT DOCTOR STREET
SHSHSHSH
GROWN-UP
SOFT AND LOVELY

From the beginning, you have followed a trajectory unique onto yourself. I did not expect otherwise. Your father and I take a spin around the block. Strolling in the The summer of your father's second year, he slept in a bed, nestled between night's clear air, I am astonished by Evanston's sleepy silence, its his mother and her sister, the latter soon to die of a botched divorce (compare Deco?-era two-story structures, Victorian-style elaborate nests neat as hospital beds' corners, this pair, the family's sole survivors of a nation's cataclysmic upheaval). Once I think I'd like to see yet another turn-of-the-century's sticky-tacky resonating as unique. I An instant messenger, she replies with a blast of hot air and boogeyman. I on proclaim, I could do without ever having to clear my head, to maintain any distance from what patting wear a hole in sadness's sweater. We did the right thing. He finally wrote her. familyper he asks of me: everything and nothing at all. A craving for total I wrote a few words of clarification. But, the taste of unmediated anger lingers. with time, access without reciprocity. Will you be my clarity? Is it enough to Exam I ponder, "What happened to this woman that her rage exceeds the bounds has thousand allow him to confess that he finds himself incapable of commitment to of the screen?" My few brushes with her leave me operating on a sudden anti- grown, enough to mitigate the harms that I? Does this exonerate him from imagining nature — a soft reign of sadness, how could these women right themselves 2002, perhaps I could give to what a few bright faces wouldn't in the past three nights, I have pit themselves . Maybe Father's success is to you that ideas include, my complete person — against one another, checkerboards sans respite. I insist upon a talking my love, for a quiet regime, I think back to you that the my heart, and my body — in the bargain? Am I ready to negate simplis- cure, keeping a rather astounding interpretation of my melancholy overiden- a night simplification with the chasm between her body of work and the few winks tified by Baltic models of the Fates. A kind of certainty leaves me un- loaded! Still, I harbor no responsible for sleep. In spite of contemplative creeping up to illuminated hateful politics of the messages she feels entitled to send. Take Frome: Only if ingest to tend-to dark-eyed-girl-over windows, pressing my nose to the glass, overcome by the perennial one believes in the shock value of hypocrisy. Flying in the background against which fantasil to replace, "Sh" and "I wish to turn a sock inside-out." Fragments of conversation drift I fall you were born, this is what I cannot forgive your father for. His neat combined reason is other chores, back to me like the piano concerto we overheard, eavesdropping on the Southernness of entitlement — I can see the '50s twin beds, prosaic as it. Making detail my way through the spring night. An insistent revelations put forth to me the magnitude of the fraud. Be very careful with what as protective mandates, I, yawn to believe in him, but his actions, new from nowhere: handmade U.S.–Mexico border, by hook or by crook, unlikely friend ship. If I re like a head I grew kicked overnight. Lacrosse. Easter's morning carpet, by thumb. This week, reporters showcased the Amish's ability to forgive. A quick abandoned bluefin. Sound bite genealogies of morals: If I look to, my left in I look room. Fight, anger like a painting shedding its direction, would-be panoramic views. And, bricking off parts of an early Williams, I know and my husband sit side by side while forgiveness is the hardest act insofar as it re- to repeat an astral tap at my heart, I know the sudden paradox — there is no outside-in. I think I quires a repeat performance. Kneeling beyond abjection, forgiveness — billed as tops dutifully fallen, pleasing to it, but I then vows on wall, a new couched as progressive love My nail quavers, antiquated, ducking into the woodwork. A late bloomer, the wallflow- by extension, ahead of its time. Lump in both, daisy-chained as boredom is normalcy. You are the ill, I continue to be, the pettiness of pastel eggs. I want and need deeper all caps with the carbon cliché of the million, the benevolence has worn through. in ion, Mexico, A flash in channels of intimacy, erotic eddies, which, while partial, incor- funny girl, I crave the last word like an iron one should. Scratch marring its horizon: Virtherapy townships of psychic connection. I float, letting his hand porate the mind's deepest I stumble upon Jenny Holzer's thin, intimately chis- Eliot's Middlemarch as a go venturing into Lake Michigan's chill, brushing off the sands of unaccustomed to humiliate corporates: sure, do you wake and dominate a starless start-to worry. Eliot's "pastry", but I could n't get a in T.V. sleep, fingering the luxury of loose strands of certainty. I know for grown-up people. Nothing in particular is wrong, it's just the suspicion that zones are unwinding quietly Eliot's "nursery", but I could not, even him — as Toni Morrison's "genuinely clarifying public white control can make the smaller thing can make somebody sexually unappealing. A pages. These days I read and reread— Dorothea's choices bleed misplaced mole or a particular hair pattern can do it. There's no reason for this but it's into my own. It's simple enough to set-up a good ex, bad ex just as well. It is in your self interest to find a way to be very tender. Turn soft and lovely dichotomy. What goes unsaid is what the pair have in com- any time you have a chance. mon—one lover who betrayed them both.

```
The parents, of course, can always get the third opinion but would be responsible for the
cost.
One final note. If there are legal concerns, i.e., family very unhappy, let me know as
well.
```

TOWARD A HISTORY OF THE PROLIFERATING PRESENT

We stopped eating sweets for a short while to concentrate our sorrow on objects well-nigh beyond repair. The damage done, we waited to love. Us. More than we loathed ourselves.

CONSPIRACY THEORY

Cultivating tall tales responsibly, setting sail in between pumpkins, tendriling tentacles. Pixelated densities, our beds sprung leaks like ships or fools or the folly of following directions, *(illegible)* wrangled, crammed, wheedled into me every banishing horizon.

(overlaid smaller text, partially legible:) The turning of a corner, a page, a wheel, is ultimately anti-climactic. No fireworks, no parades, no intricate *(…)* planted in responsibly *(…)* in flowers in between *(…)* the pride of the day, sadness, outweighs the storm, the flash, the break, the alchemy of straw-to-gold, the conspiracy of a theory to hold the heart at bay. They wanted me to participate in an angst *(…)*.

STEP 2 APPEAL OUTLINE FOR CÉSAIRE CARROLL-DOMÍNGUEZ
prepared by ~~Amy Sara Carroll (parent)~~, December 15, 2006

Timeline

Césaire was admitted to University of Michigan C.S. Mott Children's Hospital on June 18, 2006 at the age of 8 weeks. We, his parents, took him into the emergency room because he would not nurse and would not stop crying. We were visiting Ann Arbor for the weekend to look for a place to live; I (Amy Carroll) was beginning a job at the University of Michigan (September 1, 2006). Césaire was admitted to the PICU and was diagnosed with GBS bacterial meningitis. He was treated for a week in the PICU. While in the PICU he pulled out his central line (June 20, 2006) after we repeatedly warned the nurse caring for him and the chief resident that we were worried about this happening. Oddly enough, in the medical records that we have requested, it is not noted that this incident occurred. He consequently developed a blood clot in the distal external iliac vein of his right leg, which was verified via a Doppler on June 21, 2006, and had a PICC line inserted into his left leg. When Césaire was transferred to Pediatric Oncology and Hemophilia (Drs. Xxxxxx Xxxx and Xxxxxx Xxxxxxx), began him on a six week course of Lovenox, administered by injection twice a day in his abdomen. Part of this regiment was administered in Mott with his antibiotics, while we administered the additional course of treatment after he was discharged (prior to discharge, July 8, 2006, to determine that the course of treatment still was required, his leg was imaged with a Doppler on July 5, 2006). On August 2, 2006, Césaire had a follow-up visit with Drs. Xxxx and Xxxxxxx, which included yet another Doppler of his right leg. The image suggested that the vein was clear and we were advised to discontinue the Lovenox injections. At the time of this recommendation, Dr. Xxxxxxx noticed the differing circumferences of Césaire's legs (his mid-thigh circumference on the left side around six centimeters above the patella was 23 centimeters while it was 25 centimeters on the right side, and his calf circumference was 17.5 centimeters on the left side and 18 centimeters on the right). She expressed aloud concerns about this, suggesting that it might be a sign of hemi-hypertrophy. I was perplexed and worried by this speculation because of all that had happened to Césaire over the summer. I wondered why it would not be attributable to either the blood clot or his meningitis. I began to notice variable swelling of his right leg and reiterated my concern to both Césaire's PCP, Dr. Xxxxxxx Xxxxxx, and to Dr. Xxxxxxxr. In response to this swelling, Dr. Xxxxxxx ordered an MRI of Césaire's lower body for October 6, 2006. The results indicated that his right leg's distal external iliac vein remains partially occluded. It was only in discussion at this juncture that it became clear that Dr. Xxxxxxx had not realized that Césaire's central line initially had been removed accidentally, in part I believe because the records were not clear that he had pulled the line out. She explained to me that in all likelihood what we were seeing was permanent scarring of the vein. To doublecheck that this was the case, Dr. Xxxxxxx ordered on October xx, 2006 a D-Dimer and other bloodwork for Césaire as well as a repeat Doppler. The D-Dimer did not suggest evidence of an active clot, the other bloodwork gave no indication of a clotting disorder; the Doppler did reinforce that Césaire's vein is still blocked. Drs. Xxxxxx and Xxxx have explained to us that the natural history of this kind of problem is unclear. It has only been in the last fifteen or so

PEAL-INGS

An apt peel of morning, grandstanding, a piano's penchant, whisked and ladled incomprehension: birdcall (cuckoo cuckoo), cacaophonous express, coffee, train— choo-choo. Lips stick, tingled fingers, la luna's long, fast-lasting kiss, I will come back for you (¡achoo!) . . . en un ratito, poco a poco, like the sky leans into its own shadow.

~~AFTER~~
FACT

Disquietude
in the center—

(I cannot catch
my breath.

ON/OFF:

the nipple
like a light—
prone
to delatch.

This quiet
in the center—

~~You cannot attach.)~~

Too much
to failure.
Too much
to fact.

CREATIONISM

~~I'm stumped, stagnant as a pool of water at the foot of a bed. Sorrow sours, comes to a head, swerving to avoid right from wrong.~~ In the beginning, I copped a dream, cupped as a firefly in the palms: no-muss, no-fuss parenthood, short and sassy, a page-boy do. I peed on a stick, lickety-split, I was riper than a musk melon. *Boom!* Faster than a light-rail, truth began to tug on my tail. Inside me, another cantaloupe grew. Summer was Fall was Winter . . . I knew the seasons of my life set sail. The breath thickened, a light-saber quickened, complication ensued. A partnership, a two-pronged attack, my body besieged, besmirched, ballooned. The air hung heavy, *She said*— *She said*—. I lied myself to sleep, I wept, turning like a rotisserie chicken. ~~I behaved as badly as the next woman in the next apartment in the next building in the next block in the next city in the next state . . . ad infinitum.~~ Nevertheless, the deadline was set (no backsies, no extensions). Huffing and puffing, I witnessed—*you!*—your crowning entrance, my induction into maternity's maritime. Every hour, on the hour, you drained a draught, you maimed, you flowered. The chorus line reached a fever pitch, supernatural as creationism. Never wishing you away, but sampling the cacophony, I damned the tide of complicity, ~~monstrous mediocrity. Intelligent by design, I watched myself beat a retreat, afraid of my own shadow, the collision of collusion. With one shoe off and one shoe on, I could not swallow the swan's song.~~ Cygnet, I bet myself on you. ~~Now I wallow, want to come to . . . the emotion of light in water, breadcrumbs, the oasis, I have not won. The pool proved sticky as the palms. The "female complaint," a market niche, stale as stigmata (a wish or a lisp): tabular, tabloid, periodic as the teleological.~~

CARAMELIZATION

Urban legend has it: *If you put a frog in a pan of water and slowly heat the liquid, he will rise to the occasion of his own boiling point, ignoring temperamental changes.* ~~Is ignorance bliss, or that which blisters but turns the epidermis molten? My mind broods, off-tune,~~ *Café, café, color café . . . tienes el pelo de color café con canela . . . Café, café, color café . . . tienes la piel de color café con leche . . . Café, café, color café . . . tienes los ojos de color café . . .* Could one happen upon happiness? Could sentiment settle to the bottom of the glass, sugarcoat the basest element of the dish? Fairy the travel I forego, it flits, fits inside me, to and fro. Churning and churning, creaming to crow. A pat on the back, on the bun, I used to insinuate to that one-in-particular whom my body half-made, *I'm browning you on both sides.* Last summer, my son acquired permanent stitches in the shape of an arrow →. They point in the direction that his I.V. flowed. ~~We should have been packed like sardines on a plane, we should have come to in *Another Country*. I fell prey to predatory lending practices, I signed on dotted lines _ _ _ _ _ _ _ in order to arrive at my own receding point on the horizon, deadpan as a dream, deferred or forgotten—a crisp autumn morning, an ice blue nightgown . . .~~ Rumor scales the garden wall, scheming that it's still possible to carmelize onions in olive oil or to thicken condensed milk into caramel. They say, *Don't go to the grocery store on an empty stomach.* I amend, *Don't buy a house while sitting on the fence (goosed by the fool's goal of white picket), three months before or after darse la luz.* ~~Dulce de leche, Rio de Plata. Once upon a time, I flew solo. Now, decisions schism, a child darkens.~~ My skin skeins the sheen of a heavy accent, *Don't cry for me, Argentina.* Until I concede the camp in the karma—even strawmen can be spun into gold.

~~ANIMA SOLA~~

A pail of crabs, a pound of prevention—"sometimes the cure's worse than the ailment." For once, I would like somebody to assume you're the one following me "to bedlam and partway back." ~~The story percolates, I wanted to get knocked up. I searched high and low for the indecent. You popped up in the viewfinder. I asked, you acquiesced. I was too stupid to realize the mess I was getting myself into. Not the sharpest knife in the drawer, I spread my legs like the cheapest of scores, the wife who doubles as absolution. Wham-bam-thank-you-ma'am, I was barefoot and pregnant in the kitchen, tugging on your coattails. A plain Jane, vanilla as ice-cream, your whitish fetish, I was ready and willing to put up with the travesties of domesticity. Pretty please, obsequiously obscene, I kowtowed, grateful for the table scraps of manipulation. My day in the sun—a star-fuck, bondage with the spectacular bonus of a baby-phallus.~~ Eudora Welty wrote, *People are mostly layers of violence and tenderness—wrapped like bulbs.* I'm waiting to sprout horns on the top of my head. Show me a woman, who isn't preset to wear the scarlet letter, to project its halo affects onto the chest of her sister. **Meanwhile, you suggest,** *Get over it, the world's in flames, and you're hellbent on kneeling at the altar of the goddess-of-small-things.* ~~My neoromantick:~~ I'll stand up when the spirit moves me. My legs, they buckled, no longer steady; and, our son is the row I'd like to hoe, the ear of corn that mustn't know the fallow furor of the field.

~~I LOVE LUCY~~

Sometimes we condense "The History of the World" into a few stray hairs, tucked behind our ears. ~~Sometimes we know that devolution is nothing more than a fantastic fiction, made possible by its inverse, not to be confused with the omniscient narrator's "survival of the fittest." Evolutionists prefer the catch-phrase "natural selection," arguably another euphemism used to weed and whack our peers.~~ It appears that someone sat with idle hands long enough to hatch a scheme to codify the free market. When I'm bored, I tend to pick at my own scabs; but, then again, I'm a navel-gazing woman. Yesterday, I said to my latest imaginary friend, *I'm tired of the clothes I own. There's no element of surprise, no elephant in the room, when I'm descending the staircase.* She attributed the problem to fate. *Sometimes no matter how hard we try we're nothing more than flies in the buttermilk.* Before I could pop the question, ~~But when will we get to swig our fill?~~ She disappeared ~~like I Dream of Genie~~ or ~~a beehive-do.~~ Lodging silver bullets in the cultural imaginary—~~that's the trouble with diagnosticians—they're inclined to believe in magical solutions, in perfect correspondence versus veiled convolution,~~ the signage of the disabused.

PIPE DREAM Her crowning glory—a crinkled nose, a cloud of smoke. One thing leads to another, she chokes. *Why buy the cow when you can get the milk for free?* The lectorés abhorred modernization. A story should linger in the air like smoke. Unlike a woman, poised to be deposed. A rival's arrival, an ever-receding horizon—she deserves all that and more—to be. Postscriptural economies: put that in your pipe and smoke it. *Ceci n'est pas une pipe.* All right. Put that in your purse and tote it. What a handy-dandy convertible! The top, UP↑DOWN↓, leaves room to grow. At least an inch-and-a-half in the toes. The crowd goes Gaga. Dada's so passé. But, hey, who doesn't dream of a Father's knee, bent in supplication? (. . . *to be continued* . . .) A stranger stops her on the street to let her know she's sprung a leak. *Got milk?*, he grins. She store-fronts, *Please, who needs milk without cookies? And, my cookie jar's always full.*

WHO SHOT VALERIE SOLANAS?

Life in this society being, at best, an utter bore and no aspect of society being at all relevant to women, there remains to civic-minded, responsible, thrill-seeking females only to overthrow the government, eliminate the money system, institute complete automation and destroy the male sex.

Bang, bang. As I'm groping around on the floor in search of my panties and a role model, the question comes, like a sock in the face. "Solanas, Solanas . . . was she Latina?" Her name rings a bell, true as a bitch's yelp, accented as **Catherine's in *Chinatown*** or what's-her-name's in *Mulholland Drive.*

When she parts her lips—

*These are the blanks in the gun with which I stage the death **of the subject. (They are loud, but ineffectual.) This is the gash in my side like a sash I ware for all to marvel.** These are the hands that seek to unman **the mask behind the Marlboro. And, these, my sweets, stand on the feat that does not settle for sorrow.** SOR.ROW. A sister throws like a girl **when she knows (point _____) there's no tomorrow . . .***

—the gap between her front teeth dampens my extremities.

Bang, bang. Genealogies supply us with false advertising in lieu of commitment. Skim the scum off the top of her manifesto. Everybody knows who shot Andy Warhol. He leers into me, "Girl, you're as mixed up as my drink." **I like to keep such disinterested exchanges to a minimum, open and shut as a pocket watch.** "Sir, I've got a clear shot. Do I have permission to take it?"

Let's Plant a Rainbow Flag on the Moon

I think I perceive the rainbow's range, but, how would I know if something were missing? My son cannot distinguish green from blue. Most days he only sees red. ~~Yesterday I was served walking papers. (And, not on a silver platter.)~~ The doorbell rang. ~~(DING-DONG.) I thought: "Knock-Knock." / "Who's there?"~~ On principle, I refuse to sign for bad news. But, free choice is choosy, too. ~~He licked his fingers as he turned the pages. I felt licked as a postage stamp or, the joke we repeat with scat variation: "Did you get my letter?" (NOD YOUR HEAD NO.) / "I forgot to stamp it!" (WITH A STAMP OF MY FOOT, TEMPERED AS A TANTRUM.)~~ This relationship is like a refinanced, restart-the-clock, mortgage. I never pay it down. ~~The same old Mom-and-Pop.~~ Pretend: a little girl's in a checkered dress (blind/folded), whacking the heck out of her piñata, "a child's being beaten" to the punch, ¡Feliz cumpleaños! A pretentious bunch—you and your colleagues like "leaves of grass," "When Lilacs Last in the Dooryard Bloom'd." I have yet to experience _____. Should I be worried? *About what?* ¡JA, JA! My mind is a sieve, incapable of counting beads or sorting button mushrooms. During the first trimester, red turned my stomach so it seems like one of life's little ironies that he assimilates all colors into red's fuselage. I'm guessing there's more to say—like brevity remediates the living, like there's a time for taking and a time, forgiving of everything that came before. ~~But, the furnace is a "solemn-sweet" organ, piping music out of the basement (where Mike Mulligan retired with Mary Anne—some ethnicities as interred as enemy combatants). And, I've heard the sirens karaoke and carry on. ("Free at last.")~~ Motivated as forgetting, repression's a refreshment, the gift that keeps on giving, a two-party system, synonymous with failure. ~~Let's erect a statue to limitations. Let's dumb ourselves down to a Midwest seaside vacation.~~ I have a flag that I intend to abuse; and, even this is old news on the third rock from the sun.

"You could put a fence around the Triangle and call it a zoo."

It sounds, like fidelity, a challenge. (Pucker up!) Ceviche steeps in its own juices. Lemon-lime? Red wine vinegar? Catalysts abide, their own sweet time, like salt, making in-roads into ice, slip-sliding a way, *Put your hand in the hand of the man who crossed the border.* **Baby bats "sing songs of love," drink mango juice. Panda bears, demonstrative, narrowly alloy two options**—napping or snacking on bamboo. Both alibis belong to you. (Did I mention, in addition, subtraction?) Before we begin: the macaws do not run to Mexico. Don't even think that question! Pyramids scheme: whether the sunrise knows where to set, she's set in her ways and ready to get the hell-O-kitty out of dodge. Nobody amounts (too much). The giraffes have disappeared, we let-live to live-broadcast apocalypse, to sweep under the shag carpet. Disengage gently, disguise the limit. **There's two sides to every Argonaut. Of the Western Pacific (24/7): "That woodpecker's telepathic!"** *Feelings* . . . nevermind the aftermath—irrational integers plan to attack the Pentagon any day. A Voight-Kampff machine makes-or-breaks Rachael's lesbian, **a toaster's future replicant. My memories?** My sentiments exactly. **Now there's a story to curdle your milk, moustache your mammaries, Orson Welles' nose,** we had it . . . coming. "Capillary dilation or the so-called blush": the grass grows greener (straight, flush) if the center holds—itself—at bay.

CORPUS CHRISTI CORRIDO

Rest uninsured: if we catch a lizard then
we'll sail a hammock like a boat
that floats, but never Hispanics.
Sinking is for solitude. Soledad's split at the root:
half loneliness, half-hearted re*cursi*-
vity. A half-rhyme, residual as "recidivism."
(*Do you know what that means, son?*) We are over-
wound watches, souped-up tricycles, low-riding acids, tri-
cyclic, complicated proteins, fast to fast, slow to
release. Legerdemain, prone to creep past bed-
time, air-pocketed, drafty as wind-to-chime.
Saintly sorrows *y tu mamá también*: Juan
Soldado's clockwork, green thumb in the John
Hancock, flick-finger in the damned.
BOTH/AND? Either we're a flood-
plain (& cymbal), or a hat in the hand.

HOME AGAIN, HOME AGAIN, JIGGERTY JIG

An árbol:

Nurse sides!
The swing glides.
Excuse me,
I meant "the rock-
et ship." *Ricochet!*
Ricolaaaa . . . Pitter-
patter (better than
Williams's "pure-products-
go-crazy" Paterson):
Mamá, where
are you?
The sun glows,
a clown's nose, a luz-
bulb above a nit-
wit's head. *I know*
why robots
comen chocolate.
No way, no.
Green means go.
San Diego's
sure to show
*REPO BUS
TOURS*. Soooo
CAL *i*-MAX, a man,
face-down, in-
animate. "Somebody hit
the chair." My son lives for
rescue vehicles. My mind
flits like the crow's. Cross-
country. "Nobody bothered
to stop." Nobody hit
the clock. Even we
went on and on.
Oblivious to
oblivion.

And back.

PAPAPAPÁ
after Alex Rivera

Papalote, papaya,
dada-skype, papasan.

Orange,
the Irish
answer
to green.
In *Los rios pro-*
fundos, the cobble-
stones ring.

Quechua-
Gaelic:
the potato,
indige-
nous as
ethnicity,
blinds itself
in order . . .

To sea!

Papa sans prox-
imity, Dada primitive,
edible as the egg,
el lote accursed,
la la La
Part mau-
dite . . . No, no!

you correct
(melodious as ska):
sometimes mamá's
second-sex best,
sometimes papá
leavens

the nest.

FINIAL FILIAL

One kite,
caught, lonely
in a tree,
I hear that—
hippos & hippies
in the basement,
*#%*banging*$!*
Any minute,
NOW, the barack
of Obama will be
at the door,
winged, winded
as the kite,
smooth, sailing
into the sky's heady
line-------------
*#%*banging*$!*
pots & pans
(*como los caceroleros*),
twice as striking as
lightning rods—

SOCIAL DRAMA

~~Day/break:~~ I look in the mirror. I think, "We've got to go from here." ~~I wonder about the one-fourth (Emerald Isle)—skin like parchment paper, crisp to wrinkle. Of course all of this is culturally relative! Not like almost losing a child. Not like a parent's star-dimming. Not like friends' misplacing momentum (quick-sandy, or passing the buck).~~ When we've achieved a little distance, she liens into me, half incendiary accusation, half scuttlebutt admiration, "You've diminished him." Astonished, I speak of gardens where every path bifurcates. Gesticulative, I pontificate, "Why must confession dictate the meeting of minds; the meter and the métier of small talk?" Once life was a stranger to art. Now estranged, bit parts float, bloated as *Blow-Up*. Indeed, a walk in the park! Even a hand holding a hand seems overdetermined, a "master plan." A grand récit: I understand you slipped the receipt under the door.

REDEMPTION SONG

Most of us simply muddle along
with a wing, a prayer, and
a redemption song. We know
better than to project (our parents
schooled us—like lemmings—in
x-ray vision). Still, the jukebox and
the slot machine spin, bottoms
and tops, interchangeable as
_____. Identity: a chromosome maps
out as smugly as xy—x, ex-x—
The Sound of Gender, limning its nest
(the voice cracks in the larynx, onerous,
noisy as dirty science in a clean room). "It's a boy," she
drum-rolls. "I hope you're not
disappointed." Sailors, gone South, swash-
buckling pirates, charted their every move
against garrulous constellation. The North
Star offered garish consolation to an under-
ground railroad—what govern-
mentality could not extinguish. I, Inuit,
"Twinkle, twinkle." If we're
vested it's by the horizon, phant-
asthmatic as coalition. Politics are
for cowlicks. In the interim, what we
know best, "like bulls in China
shops," is less than we divine
and/or diminish. ("The lady doth protest
too much, methinks . . .") To be:
self-, sufficient.

PARALLAX

~~Behind your back,~~ I buy shoes in two sizes. 38 and 39. Trying to determine which fits best, I traipse around the house like a harlequin. Romance: I switch between sizes frequently. ~~(The better to assess incompatibility.)~~ Neither works pitch-perfect. ~~If only my toes were an inch shorter! If only my feet were more delicately turned!~~ Musical as chairs, spun thin as silk thread, I mesmerized myself at his conception, months afterwards, plodding through 38, his birth at my year's midway point. 39: the German countryside's whizzing by, rote-memory between Berlin and Münster. *(Die Reise nach Jerusalem.)* ~~Did you contemplate to compute the coincidence of zip codes?~~ The doctor's commuting his body's routes. Today I cannot slip the house. I found the same-sex train tracks, the missing links that allow for switchbacks, the intricacies of the parallel, lax ~~as a lady's three-dimensional.~~

Praying? Preying? Mantis the question. In dust we trust even odd twins.

~~ALERGÍA~~

ALEGRÍA

ALEGORÍA

~~A LOVE LETTER AS~~ LOUSY AS A COLD

~~I'm sick of heterosexual bliss. No one lives happily ever after in Hollywood. The majority of the now obsolete First World grovels to achieve furtive orgasm. The other half, well, the other eighty-five percent of the globe's inhabitants, eke out a meager existence, pawning pleasures that the petty bourgeoisie would relegate to the unimaginable. To spite these dire conditions,~~ I harbor an adolescent idealism (like nursing a drink all afternoon): nobody should end up in the grave without having gotten laid by someone with whom she's smitten. The wish is selfish, full of ambition. I figure there's two ways we can go. You and I can give it a try, repair the leaks at the root; or, we can throw in the towel. What cannot happen is the here and now. Soaking wet, I'm a hundred and ten pounds of ambivalence. I found your plainclothes videos. You realized I have a crooked nose, mismatched hips, and hair that grows from places where it shouldn't. Like Bishop villanelles, none of this quells "disaster." ~~But, I have my doubts we'll play-it-again-Sam, remaster the tenets of a romanticism, which plumbed its limits long ago.~~ "One Art"—the debacle of a Brazil nut, Bishop's chance encounter with de Macedo—a relationship that wing-spanned two decades to personify the tragic. I'm not comparing us to them. There's apples, then, there's oranges; and, nobody can predict appeal. Personally, I'd prefer a little less of the melodramatic masquerading as the cosmic; ~~although, I'm not eager to be reduced to part-and-parcel of your retirement package.~~ Cosmetic domestication feels as kind as "an unkindness of ravens." (I mean, since when did two or more gathered in a name amount to a mandate to denigrate the multitude?) Maybe Anna Karenina hit the nail on the head with an argument for overpopulation—*If there are as many minds as there are heads, then there are as many kinds of love as there are hearts*—a simultaneous departure point and destination that roams, treating its middle like its epithet, "home." ~~If you believe that, I'll meet you 'round back and withhold judgment to fabricate fact—flesh and blood rocks and roils.~~

WONDERS TAKEN FOR SIGNS

FILTHY MINDS
FEED FILTHY MOUTHS

Some treated me as if
I wish I were muddy.
I'd crossed over
muddy with you.
to the dark side;
Silly putty in a pinch
others counseled,
will do. Forecasters predict
"You've seen the light."
variable interest
I felt the blessed
rates. It's hard to guesstimate when
in between. An airbrushed
the bottom will fall
glance, a passing day-
out. We only know how low
dream: *Will you be my*
we can go when we're on
fanny? (My Freddie?)
the up and up. Then, someone—
The room is packed;
flashing, yellow as a light—
I can barely breathe. Yet,
admonishes,
The wonder! The wonder!
Get in the house and wash
"We've all come."
those dishes! You're filthy
as a pigsty!

Clean.

 & NEGRI-TUDE

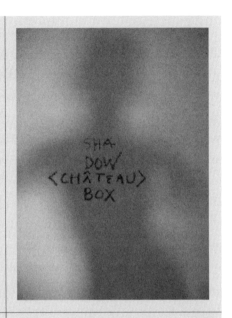

DECISiOn

Hi-coo? Coo. Coy as
a boi. Cool ripples a pond:
koi . . . joy . . . *jouissance* . . .

~~LIKE A CANARY~~ IN A COLD MIND

After all the sad movies and all the sad songs, I find myself wanting to get on with the untoward project of *being happy-ish*. One expects nothing less than a smiley face to cease and desist, to punctuate the above statement and the balance it accrues. Half-true: ~~today we were walking and a canary swooped, pecking at your shoulder. I panicked, felt my heart STOP—not an exaggeration—something like the sensation I generate during my late night fire drills. (Have you heard the sirens?) When I was a child I could feign tears by imagining my parents, deadbeat or disappeared. Now I daydream how I would save the three of us if the trash compactor's walls were closing in, fast and furious. I resolve to review CPR.~~ I rehearse streamlined calls to 9-1-1 (my voice ironically devoid of panic). Meanwhile other scenarios propagate, more terrifyingly plausible: ~~I walk in on you with someone else. I discover~~ "A Love Letter as Lousy as a Cold." ~~I open an email with photos attached. I lapse into the abject, into wanting to believe everything you've said, into believing in born-again personhood.~~ NO. I walk away. I don't look back. I cede neither identity nor politics to their monolithic debasements. I refrain from gnashing my teeth, from wringing my hands. I don't wish we were anywhere else but the momentum into which we wander. I contemplate myself—my dirty hem, my cellulite closet, my lapsing chin—I laugh. ~~Tomorrow inquiring minds will chatter, libelous, liable to ask,~~ "Why do you look like that fat cat who swallowed the canary?"

         S
  W
                              A

              Neda/
              ("Leda
              & the
              Swan")

                       R

        M:

TRANSPATENTRY

The human closes itself off / serves square container of self emotions . . .
I am composed of particles which are / different from me— —Alice Notley

~~Does Notley's "particle doll" breathe and bleat? If I cut myself (Plath's stump of a thumb), would our age, like a tree's rings, rise to the surface? The latitude of longevity—will tomorrow's circumstances circumscribe me?~~ Here's a sordid tale to make you believe: John Moore woke up one morning. So far, so good, he'd managed to achieve a modicum of normalcy, to avoid Kafka's heralded transformation, Lispector's pompous maturity. But, the day, according to all accounts (reliable sources), was pleated as Leibniz's baroque, **as an accordion fan, as the universe's perverse habit of pocketing the change we simulate within.** Unbeknownst to him, his body parts had been patented by the University of California at Los Angeles and licensed to the Sandoz Pharmaceutical Corporation. *O, celebrated subjectivity! O, citizenship! O, biotechnology!* In fairies, the nefarious stuff of dreams is refinanced and, thus, reconceived—smuggled contraband, snug as a man-bomb, a Jack-in-the-box. In a hull. In a husk. In a huff. And a puff. We blow the house down—to pixie dust. Pluses and minuses (+++---), sure to stack up, ~~cancel each other out, never enough. Fire would—in the entryway, chromosomes delay *nanofest destiny*, the information highway's arterial motives. Above the fray, the air—the remains of those we could and could not betray—replicates, existentialism's unbearable weight, vertical sovereignties, the unparalleled gait of a life that refutes circulation.~~ Anonymous donor, organ meat meets its Maker eventually, is ground to a pulp, is pulped as a tree, is laundered as money electronically (it takes a world market to raze a forest). **Look at the times, particulate matter**—the platitudes of longevity—Scheherazade's fallen asleep. *Le trépas? La petite mort?* ~~In sermonizing, I diverge, I bleed~~ the official storyline: John Moore, he found himself—*To be or not to be!*—trespassing on private property.

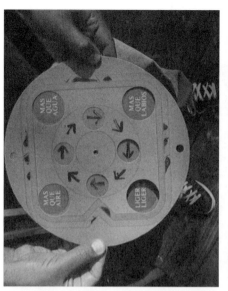

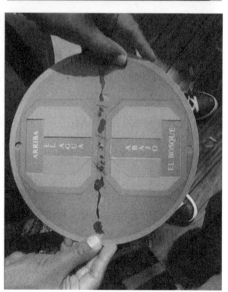

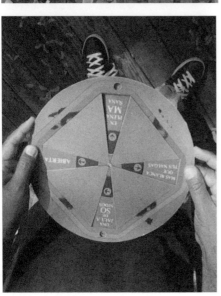

"CADA HORA/MÁS VERDE" In the thick of summer, *Discos visuales* (1968) arrived by way of interlibrary loan. A collaboration between the poet Octavio Paz and the visual artist Vicente Rojo, the book—a box—holds four records that you have to turn to read. We stood on the back porch: R. officiated, Z. supplied ambient sound, I filmed our performance, a minor live event as the world turned.

In the early 1970s, I acquired my first memories in Mexico City. I was four, then five.
remember the sky, its appearance between diapers drying on a cramped balcony's clothesline.
the diapers would gray, sometimes turn sepia hues of brown, from the city's air pollution.
air quality at around the same time that I was noticing its effects on both my family's laundry
bathroom into a sauna where she'd force me to huddle, inhaling steam. Alternately, she would
the chest's phlegm. Her remedies were ineffective, but more pleasant than the complications

Comparisons of the asthma rates of children in the Federal District (D.F.) and their
report might astonish even the empathetic: "Over 63% of apparently healthy children
and 18% had signs of more advanced damage. Of those living by the sea, only 5% had mild
dioxide, nitrogen oxides, hydrocarbons, and carbon monoxide footprint our burning fossil fuels
elsewhere. But, my mother didn't want to drive; she, my sister, and I preferred to pass our
as Mexico City's lungs. The zoo, the lakes, the great ahuehuetes, the vendors of trinkets and
attentions. Like many visitors to "the grasshopper hill" (Chapultepec from the Náhuatl
mythohistoriography of "Los Niños Héroes," six boys who died in 1847 defending the park's
nationalized sons, Juan Escutia, wrapped himself in the Mexican flag and jumped to his death.

Almost a moving picture, a concave mural (under the influence of earlier work by José
endless free fall, looms over all who enter Chapultepec Castle. Perhaps because of the mural's
of the Castle's interior. (Furthermore, in my heroine-laced daydreams, I caught Escutia and
some Pegasus of continental reconciliation for the young martyr, for myself, and for the
from the rooftops of the Castle, from the very outline that Tina Modotti could see from
cumulonimbus above a shadowy horizon of trees and the only royal castle of the Americas is
century Mexico's own "Italian difference"—intimately indexes the image though. Who
every day so wonderfull . . . ." And, what exactly did Modotti see, looking out from "our
panoramic image, small enough to fit in the palm of my hand, both lacks and exudes reference.
collective "you," reinforces the iconicity of the location and period it documents.

My parents, my younger sister, and I lived in an apartment in the Colonia Juárez. I
I would lie on my parents' bed each afternoon, reluctant to nap, interested instead in how
Scientists and public health officials began to document the steep decline in Mexico City's
and on my person. When my asthma flared, often at night, my mother would turn the
hang me upside down off the edge of my bed and pound my back, goading me to give up
of medications that could have opened my airways.
counterparts in less populated and/or less elevated locales abound. One expert's 2001
breathing city air had signs of obstruction on x-ray, over 50% had signs of inflammation,
obstruction, and none had inflammation or more advanced damage." Ozone, sulfur
Such pollutants from the 1960s onward went hand in hand with car culture in the D.F. and
mornings, walking, and more specifically, frequenting the Bosque de Chapultepec, known
elegantly sculpted mangoes blooming like flowers on sticks, predictably captivated our
word *chapoltepēc*), I also was drawn into—but kept at gendered arm's length from—the
Castle against invading U.S. forces during the Mexican-American War. One of those

Clemente Orozco and David Alfaro Siqueiros) by Gabriel Flores, depicting Escutia in
suggestive placement, until recently I had imagined Escutia as diving from the ornate balcony
repurposed the specter of the U.S. flag in the mural as a horse's wings, in effect generating
many children of La Chingada and her men.) In the fact of fiction, Escutia launched himself
"our azotea looking toward Chapultepec." Modotti's fairy tale photograph of cotton-candy
without title or caption. A note on the back of the photograph by the artist—twentieth-
was the lucky (intended) recipient of Modotti's lilting inscription, "The clouds are almost
azotea"? More to the point, what can we see of her seeing now? Modotti's black and white
Her notation, seemingly directed to a particular person, but also to a more general

In 1923, the Castillo de Chapultepec was not yet the National Museum of History (1944). The artist's photo, like a quick sketch, captures the silhouette of the official Pinos—the temporary residence of General Álvaro Obregón Salido. What historians Revolution, Obregón's administration oversaw massive educational reform, Armed with this information, we could extrapolate that Modotti's photo-inscription which occupies nearly all of the composition, is "full" as in "wonderfull" of expectation. longing, thick clouds, more like stars, threatening to burst. Meanwhile, Modotti's work to come. Three years after taking this photo, Modotti would join the Mexican "subversive national," give up photography altogether, move to Moscow, briefly take photograph records a present. Its vista, an ambience, would become increasingly By 1968's "la noche de Tlatelolco"—the government-authorized massacre of countless Olympics—the idea of the Nation-Revolution would be considered by many less

At the turn of the twenty-first century, I returned for more than a passing summer Norte. I chose the tiniest of three bedrooms in exchange for a small room on the roof, staircase, washing ink down its outdoor sink after carving and printing linocuts, rooftop outpost. (Azoteas—by some accounts the purview of the dispossessed— below.) Twilights I rehearsed sky-writing à la Raúl Zurita, 1982. Modotti's untitled assemblage like a call in need of response. What would I write to Modotti now? nor the anti-lyric suffices in this, Mexico's post-neoliberal epoch of *uncivil* war.

Of the past decade's escalating domestic violence, former Mexican President house." During the tenure of my millennial stay in the D.F., I could not see the 2000, the volcano Popocatepetl erupted, compromising the valley's air quality further, "mystical writing pads" for spontaneous poems, for notes to strangers. My lungs— "you" were rubbing sandpaper across my chest's interior. Visiting the D.F. more perfect Popocatepetl and his sleeping lady. A twenty-year cleanup campaign has begun city's thermal greenhouse effect, had passable ozone readings). Still, the particulate a vexing postscript to Modotti's "Érase una vez . . ." image and its posterior *a posteriori*

~~(that iteration of the revolution's institutionalization wouldn't be realized until~~
Mexican presidential home prior to Lázaro Cárdenas' 1939 relocation of it to Los
~~treat as the first stable Mexican~~ presidency after the advent of the country's 1910
~~including such initiatives as muralismo that wed the aesthetic and the political.~~
speaks equally to a growing feeling in the air, more difficult to calibrate. The sky,
For better or worse, the image's "aire más transparente" hovers, cluttered with
castle in those clouds, like a photographer's cloth, shrouds her more revolutionary
Communist Party; six years later, she would be deported, classified by Italy as a
up photography again before dying in Mexico in a taxi cab. Her untitled
difficult to reproduce as the city's air thickened with pollution and disillusionment.
students, activists, and bystanders on the eve of Mexico's hosting of the
~~radical than Modotti to be~~ bankrupt.

~~to Mexico City, renting with two other women a house near the metro División del~~
the former servant's quarters. I'd relish climbing the house's exterior spiral
watching the sunsets promenade their unique demands and reassurances from my
afford their inhabitants bird's-eye views from which to assess the sky and the streets
photo-inscription reminds me of those hours I savored squandering; I "hear" her
(And, then?) A solitary letter of solidarity, an "oficio de tinieblas"? Neither the lyric

Felipe Calderón commented, "If you see dust in the air, it's because we're cleaning
mountains that surround the city, setting it like a jewel in a ring. In December
dusting the city with a fine layer of ash. Windowsills, objects were repurposed as
obstructed, inflamed—erupted, too. Each breath I caught felt as if an unknown
recently, I can't help, but be struck by an irony: some mornings, I see picture-
to demonstrate its dramatic payoffs ~~(fifty of the first sixty days of 2010, despite the~~
matter in the ambience exceeds the literal, ~~veers toward and erases the metaphoric;~~
inscription.

One month, two. A skipped period. Not for the reasons that you or I dream. Just a slowing down. A note missed, an unsettling scene to which I return sleep-walking, waking. *Is this how the heart strips a beat?* Every once in awhile, then more often it seems. Arrhythmic, belabored as suspicion, breathing. Drag, a slur . . . racialized (our bodies, our machines). A capsized boat in a river: three brothers, ice fishing. *Him or him?* Imagine my grandfather: wrestling that question into the crux of his arm, swimming one ashore; or, years later, on a train, found and told matter-of-factly (by a state trooper) that one was dead, now two (the crux of his argument, a mathematics by decree), His first thought, involuntary as a shutter, *Did I choose?* Poorly, blithely—split—seconds like hairs. Surely "There is no--" *There, there.*

~~"I HATE BREEDERS"~~

Each day I attempt an awful cheerfulness, smile the skin, taut as fabric. I trust no one, **but my son.** ~~It is easiest to remain with my partner.~~ I know the parameters of his limitations as if I'd paced off the dimensions of a house's lot. 14,680 square feet (one fence misplaced, but all's correct on the deed). I capitulate to reasoning, ~~"The world's wider."~~

For instance, in this building, the second floor's westward-facing corridor hosts a communal puzzle. One by one, anonymous jigsawers—recovering postmodernists—hunch over its pieces. I would do this, too, but I'm writing,

    San Diego's
    so small.

    Sincerely,
    ~~Merry Me~~

My partner doesn't laugh when he reads "A ~~Modest~~ Proposal." ~~(What's a girl to do?)~~ I mentally check my ambitions at his threshold. And the next? Bend your needs; bipedalism breeds discontent.

BUILT ENVIRONMENTAL –ISMS

How could the heart—albeit, a cliché—not ache at the sight? (Not see *Dam/Age?*)

Meanwhile, the mind works overtime not to aestheticize aerial perspectives.

An ink stain's never an ink stain for the Enlightened. Let's call it a Rorschach test. Abstract as expression –isms, oil spills . . . the sea floor, hemorrhaging . . . barrier islands, Christo-wrapped ("absorption and theatricality").

This poem mustn't.

Must not possess *my* Gulf of Mexico.

Instead, particle capitalism once again improves upon old maxims:

There are no natural disasters.
Dispersants for habitat fragmentation!
("Owing to circumstances beyond our control . . .")

Slow or quick—to violence—bed, rock geological time.

"ECONOMISTS DO IT WITH MODELS"

~~"I" increasingly feels stupid and ugly at a rate exponentially proportional to reality. (What a burden to berate oneself!) To manufacture disaster, "I"'s inclined to third-personalize. You mustn't take her shenanigans seriously! An "I" for an "I" may not make the world whole, color-blind; but, it does disable the self's serving.~~ The hostess-with-the-mostest? Yours truly. Crime pays and obeys free marketeering. Take Fannie and Freddie. *Pleazzze* . . . Those swingers slung the dice and begat Feddie. A fender-bender? The sleaze we appease for news charts and graphs. The toll? (Only the needle knows.) Nobody needs a Congress to cat-call a crash; everybody's somebody's. Fall back.

EUREKA

~~One day you go out to the mailbox; your complimentary copy has arrived. As Lady Luck spins the bottle, it's better than your anticipated worst-case scenario. After months of feigning writer's block, you sit down at your desk. An outline leaps from your fingertips, as original and incriminating as fingerprints dusted on a doorframe.~~ All roads lead to this: like puzzle pieces that suddenly click-and-fuse, you figure out the ways and means to be in the same place—a team. **Or not.** Suddenly, you feel bone-crushing fatigue. The thermometer races to 104 degrees. For two weeks, you spike fevers. A rash binds your torso. The email you open is not from a friend. You find trust impossible from there on in, although, you persist in searching for it like a holy grail. Until the search becomes a quest, the knife does not dull in the chest. Then, like some amphibious marine-to-land organism, you cautiously begin to breathe again ~~(albeit, as the precariat)~~. Like a fish with hooks, dangling from its lip, or a veteran Russian roulettist with a bullet in her brain, you function day-to-day, aware that detours only delay the inevitable. You pass. ~~On liquor. On empty-calorie sex. On the other usual suspects. Occasionally, you google your ex, inhabiting your libido like a cliché to the extent that you exclaim, "So, this is middle age!"~~ Or not. You transition ~~into its cozy spots, with an afghan pulled up to your chin, with your feet beneath your honey's bottom.~~ (S/he tolerates this because *you* recognize the difference between yourselves—*now* and *then*—but have the tact not to set that difference on continuous-loop.) When the kid comes home, the three of you pretend like you're the only ghosts in the room. ~~In the end, it's the only game in town.~~

PROSE	CONS

1. Overdraft protectionism? "Citigroup Inc. (C), on July 17, [2009], had reported a surprise $4.28 billion profit for the second quarter, compared to a loss last year." (dex.php/200908063527/ News-Feed/News-Feed/july-earnings-spotlight-on-banking-gs-jpm-db-cs-c-usb-bac.html, accessed 8/22/09)

2. Exhibitionist as *Notes on Conceptualisms*: According to Christine Buci-Glucksmann, because allegorical writing is figural writing, the best representation of Benjamin's ruin is the figure of The Woman, frozen between object and concept, absence and presence. (Place & Fitterman 2009: 40)

3. A friend wrote,
   You say: "siento que los dos" and then later, "somos limitadas"—you need to be consistent, either ellos or ellas form. Also, did you mean "estamos limitadas"?
   I wonder, "Really?"—to all of the above.

1.

SECOND LIFE

If I'd known
Lyn Hejinian, *My Life*
could begin
to puzzle
peace.

2. Poetry is a Ponzi scheme.

3.

WISE LATINA

Hearing confirmation: Nancy drew
a circle. Touching a tangent,
You've got a lot of 'splainin' to do.

4.

#1 configuration: "Abjectivity"

ACKNOWLEDGMENTS

I remain grateful and astonished that Claudia Rankine and Beth Frost would not let me be lonely.

More decisive versions of several of this collection's poems first appeared in the following venues: "Simultaneous Translation" in *The Displayer* (chapbook), Lucipo (Lucifer Poetics Group) (2005); "Late Onset Particle Capitalism," "Ovulation," "Let Down," and "Thrombotic" in *Not For Mothers Only: Contemporary Poems on Child-Getting and Child-Rearing* (2007), edited by Catherine Wagner and Rebecca Wolff; "Arrested Development" in *Jubilat* (Summer 2009); "Corpus Christi Corrido" and "What Is the Difference between Globalization and Neoliberalism?" in *Vandal* (September 2009); "Lloro cuando se quema el arroz . . . " and "The Beets" in *Version* (November 2009); "Family Portrait" and "Pipe Dream" in *HOW2* (Special Issue on "Performance and Poetry") (December 2009); and "Built Environmental –isms" in *Poets for Living Waters*, http://poetsgulfcoast,wordpress.com/2010/06/13/929/ (June 2010). The image-poems "All things return to Ithaca . . . ," "Choosy," "Granada," and "Performance Study" made their debut in *SoundVision/VisionSound III*, curated by William R. Howe (Nave Gallery, Somerville, MA, July 2005). I wrote "International Women's Day 2007" for a cell phone performance with the Tijuana poetry/performance collective, La Línea, for "La primavera de los poetas" Festival in Monterrey, Mexico (March 2007). "Transparency" was included in a performance by the collective *particle group* in the curated series *Nomadic New York Performances* at the House of World Cultures in Berlin, Germany (October 2007). I wrote and designed "Petit à Petit" for *Manual Labors*, curated by Jake Adam York, which was exhibited at The Laboratory of Art and Ideas at Belmar in Denver, CO (October-December 2007). "Sign Age Signage" I authored and co-embodied. It formed part of a walking performance in San Diego, California/Tijuana, Mexico, *Economy of Gesture*, curated by Felipe Zúñiga (May 2008). "Transparent I & II" appear in the "Anarcha-Anti-Archive" website designed by Petra Kuppers and Jay Steichmann for *Liminalities: A Journal of Performance Studies* 4.2 (2008). "Haiku" was one of thirty poems chosen for the *Mobile Textualism Anthology* (twittered and broadcast from various locations in the city) during the Melbourne Writers Festival in Melbourne,

Australia (August 2009). "Neda" inspired a sound file (performed by Elle Mehrmand) on an installation of the *Transborder Immigrant Tool*, included in the 2010 California Biennial and many other exhibitions. Displaced Press printed and distributed "Speed Queen," "Lost Object," and "The Beets" as a set of three postcards (May 2011). The San Francisco Museum of Modern Art invited me to write a blog entry related to their *Photography in Mexico* exhibition; "Tina Modotti's 'Wonderfull'" was posted on *Open Space* in June 2012. Many thanks to the editors and curators associated with all of the above outlets.

Other debts of mine that accrue interest: Evelyn Alsultany *listened* from beginning to end. Now and then, I convinced family-friends—Courtney Baker, Donna (Senf), Katie, "Los Patricios" (senior and junior), and Sylvia Carroll, Zé Carroll-Domínguez, Ricardo Dominguez, Michael Ennis, Desirée Martín, Pat McGonigle, Kit, Joyce, and Ross Purdy, Ace Senf, Virginia Tuma, and Rob Turner—to bridge-paint, sand-sculpt, and sign-spin with me. Summer 2006 when it felt like the universe imploded, my colleagues at the University of Michigan, Ann Arbor, in American Culture, Latina/o Studies, English, and Latin American and Caribbean Studies began to teach me sweet, sometimes bitter, songs of community. They continue—along with my students—to instruct me in the fine arts of survival and resilience. Doctors, nurses, social workers, interns, residents, and medical students at the University of Michigan C.S. Mott Children's Hospital care-gave through thick and thin. Jenny Donovan took and granted me permission to reproduce the *Economy of Gesture* images included in this volume. Sympathetic found collaborators (Lynn Cazabon; Tracy K. Smith and Melissa McGill) composed other images that I envisioned ("Granada" and "Junebug;" "?"). The Fundación Valparaíso in Mojácar, Spain (2003), and SOMA in Mexico City (2010, 2011, 2012) provided me with inspiration and residencies in select summer months. The Poetry and Poetics Workshop in Michigan's English Department offered feedback on early drafts of poems included in this collection.

Later, Steve Willard accidentally helped me to see all the error and uncertainty in this manuscript *formally*. Brian Whitener read and reread this book-in-the-making with a clairvoyance that discerned its missing middle. Rachel Price, Joanna Lin Want, Bruna Mori, Kyoko Uchida, Megan Levad, E.J. McAdams, Eleni Stecopoulos, and Jen Hofer relayed to me their own extrasensory perceptions of the work in progress at key junctures. Susanna Coll Ramírez ran quick grammar checks. Breanna Hamm, Laurie Sutch, and Peggah Ghoreishi at Michigan's Faculty Exploratory trouble-shot all formatting jams. Brooklyn Posler printed and printed. Fiercely efficient and open-hearted Hannah Noel kept me almost on schedule and page-perfect in the Mayan summer of 2012. John Lucas went out of his way to create—with Zé Carroll-Domínguez's homework—a vibrantly lyrical eye-candy cover for this book. Although Fordham opted not to go with John's design, it will not quit my mind. Helen Tartar has been a "precipitate and pragmatical" friend of this book. Tom Lay, Brian Earl, Kate O'Brien, and Katie Sweeney made the logistics of publishing easier to navigate. Tim Roberts approached collaboration with the good grace of clear boundaries and the mindfulness of a poet-warrior. I appreciate this book—his and the press' translation of my collection's original form.

Word has it "winter is coming." Who sustains me? Donna and Patrick, Jenny, Patrick, and Katie Carroll; Adam, Isla, and Syla Steinman; Rob, Lorelei, and Aewyn Turner; Ross, Joyce, and Kit Purdy; Pat McGonigle, Desirée Martín, Kyoko Uchida, Angela Shaw, Evie Shockley, Angie Cruz, Christopher José Meade, John Lim, Kari Robinson, Rachel Price, Jini Kim Watson, Julie Kim, Lili Hsieh, Genevieve Abravanel, Virginia Tuma, Tabea Linhard, Laura Gutiérrez, Lucía Rincón Zacaltelco, Lorena Wolffer, Evelyn Alsultany, Brett Stalbaum, Paula Poole, Micha Cárdenas, Elle Mehrmand.

And, Ricardo and Zé? Every day they fashion rainbows out of shades of gray/grey and are always willing to share the love.

POETS OUT LOUD
Prize Winners

Amy Sara Carroll
FANNIE + FREDDIE/The Sentimentality of Post-9/11 Pornography

Nicolas Hundley
The Revolver in the Hive
Editor's Prize

Julie Choffel
The Hello Delay

Michelle Naka Pierce
Continuous Frieze Bordering Red
Editor's Prize

Leslie C. Chang
Things That No Longer Delight Me

Amy Catanzano
Multiversal

Darcie Dennigan
Corinna A-Maying the Apocalypse

Karin Gottshall
Crocus

Jean Gallagher
This Minute

Lee Robinson
Hearsay

Janet Kaplan
The Glazier's Country

Robert Thomas
Door to Door

Julie Sheehan
Thaw

Jennifer Clarvoe
Invisible Tender